TOP **10**
NEW ORLEANS

PAUL GREENBERG

EYEWITNESS TRAVEL

Left **Figurines at NOMA** Center **Canal streetcar** Right **Rhinos at Audubon Zoo**

LONDON, NEW YORK,
MELBOURNE, MUNICH AND DELHI
www.dk.com

Printed and bound in China by
Leo Paper Products Ltd
First American Edition, 2010
12 13 14 15 10 9 8 7 6 5 4 3 2 1
Published in the United States by
DK Publishing, 375 Hudson Street,
New York, New York 10014

**Copyright 2010, 2012 © Dorling Kindersley
Limited, London, A Penguin Company**

Reprinted with revisions 2012

All rights reserved. Without limiting the rights
under copyright reserved above, no part of this
publication may be reproduced, stored in or
introduced into a retrieval system, or
transmitted in any form or by any means
(electronic, mechanical, photocopying,
recording, or otherwise), without the prior
written permission of both the copyright owner
and the above publisher of this book.

Published in Great Britain by Dorling Kindersley
Limited. A catalog record for this book is
available from the Library of Congress.

ISSN 1479-344X
ISBN 978 0 7566 8551 5

Within each Top 10 list in this book, no hierarchy
of quality or popularity is implied. All 10 are, in
the editor's opinion, of roughly equal merit.

Floors are referred to throughout in accordance
with American usage; ie the "first floor" is at
ground level.

MIX
Paper from
responsible sources
FSC™ C018179
www.fsc.org

Contents

New Orleans' Top 10

The information in this DK Eyewitness Top 10 Travel Guide is checked regularly.
Every effort has been made to ensure that this book is as up-to-date as possible at the time
of going to press. Some details, however, such as telephone numbers, opening hours, prices,
gallery hanging arrangements and travel information are liable to change. The publishers
cannot accept responsibility for any consequences arising from the use of this book, nor
for any material on third party websites, and cannot guarantee that any website address in
this book will be a suitable source of travel information. We value the views and suggestions
of our readers very highly. Please write to: Publisher, DK Eyewitness Travel Guides,
Dorling Kindersley, 80 Strand, London, Great Britain WC2R 0RL, or email: travelguides@dk.com.

Cover: Front – **Alamy Images**: Martin Thomas Photography bl; **Alex Demyan**: main.
Spine – **Alamy Images**: JG Photography b; Back – **Alamy Images**: Steve Hamblin tl; **Dorling Kindersley**:
Helena Smith tc; **Photolibrary**: Tips Italia/Marvin Newman tr.

Left **Float at Mardi Gras World** Center **Mississippi Riverfront** Right **Café Degas, Mid-City**

Left **Street musicians, Jackson Square** Right **St. Louis Cathedral in Jackson Square**

Key to abbreviations
Adm *admission charge* **Ave.** *avenue* **St.** *street*

NEW ORLEANS' TOP 10

NEW ORLEANS' TOP 10

TOP 10 New Orleans' Highlights

One of the most popular tourist destinations in the United States, New Orleans winds gracefully in a crescent shape around a bend in the Mississippi River. The city has a rich French and Spanish cultural history, evident in its food, architecture, and customs. It is known for its historical jazz tradition, colorful festivities, and an unmatched joie de vivre. Nicknamed "the City that Care Forgot," New Orleans is renowned for its carefree vibe.

New Orleans Museum of Art

Founded a century ago by Isaac Delgado, a sugar broker, the New Orleans Museum of Art boasts a collection of more than 40,000 objects *(right)* in 46 galleries, valued at more than $200 million *(see pp8–11)*.

Audubon Zoo

This site has sheltered animals *(left)* since 1884. Considered among the best in the country, it covers 58 acres (23 ha) and houses animals in their natural habitats *(see pp12–13)*.

Royal Street

This street *(above)* is the highlight of the French Quarter. Royal Street offers the best fine art in the city, as well as antiques and gourmet restaurants *(see pp14–17)*.

Aquarium of the Americas

This aquarium *(left)* is one of the finest in the country. A top attraction in New Orleans, the state-of-the-art facility houses 15,000 sea animals, and interactive displays on marine life *(see pp18–19)*.

Preceding pages **Creole cottages, Upper French Quarter**

Mardi Gras 6
Billed as the world's largest street party, Mardi Gras is an annual spring celebration that culminates on Fat Tuesday (just before Lent). This colorful festival, associated with feasting and parties, marks the last celebration before Lent *(see pp22–3)*.

5 Mississippi Riverfront
New Orleans is bordered by the Mississippi *(above)*. Take a streetcar ride alongside it, dine by the river, or board a steamboat for a leisurely dinner cruise *(see pp20–21)*.

7 Jackson Square
Located in the center of the French Quarter, Jackson Square *(left)* was the main square of old New Orleans. Today, it is an attractive park with St. Louis Cathedral as a backdrop and beautiful architecture all around *(see pp24–5)*.

8 New Orleans City Park
This park *(above)* is New Orleans' version of Central Park in New York. It is a lush landscaped space with dozens of attractions. The park is a popular getaway from the urban bustle *(see pp26–7)*.

9 Bourbon Street
Bourbon Street *(left)* features some of the French Quarter's main attractions, including beautiful hotels, excellent vintage restaurants and bars, and plenty of live jazz. This is a must-see for visitors *(see pp28–9)*.

1000 ⌐———— yards ¬ 0 ⌐ meters ————⌐ 1000

Canal Street 10
Ride the streetcar *(right)*, enjoy an outdoor lunch, shop at fine boutiques, or try your luck at Harrah's New Orleans Casino on the widest boulevard in the world *(see pp30–31)*.

☰10 New Orleans Museum of Art

The New Orleans Museum of Art – more commonly known as NOMA – is one of the pre-eminent centers of fine arts in the Gulf South. NOMA is an educational center, a family destination, a popular tourist attraction, and the centerpiece of New Orleans' elegant City Park (see pp26–7). Its permanent collections and rotating exhibits rival the best museums in the country. The museum is also a community social center, frequently hosting high-profile weddings, receptions, fundraisers, and social events. Situated near the entrance to New Orleans City Park, the museum is a historic landmark.

Elegant facade of the New Orleans Museum of Art

🚋 Take the Canal streetcar to the main entrance of the City Park, and walk down the grand promenade to the museum.

🍴 Located just outside the museum, the Parkview Café, serves sandwiches, salads, desserts, soft drinks, and ice cream. Visitors can also use the free Wi-Fi here.

• 1 Diboll Circle, New Orleans City Park
• Map H2
• 504-488-2631
• Open 10am–5pm Tue–Sun (to 9pm Fri)
• Adm $10 for adults, $8 for seniors and students, $6 for children
• www.noma.org
• Canal streetcar
• Sydney & Walda Besthoff Sculpture Garden: 10am–4:45pm daily (until dusk Wed)

Top 10 Features

1. Sydney & Walda Besthoff Sculpture Garden
2. Arts Quarterly
3. NOMA Photography Collection
4. Contemporary Art
5. Special Exhibitions
6. Café NOMA
7. Wellness Classes in the Sculpture Garden
8. Where Y'Art
9. Museum Shop
10. Annual Odyssey Ball

1 Sydney & Walda Besthoff Sculpture Garden

This beautifully landscaped garden *(above)* features an outdoor collection of more than 60 sculptures, most of which were donated by the Besthoff Foundation. Works by Henry Moore, George Segal, and Barbara Hepworth are featured here.

2 Arts Quarterly

Four times a year, NOMA publishes and distributes this acclaimed full-color magazine. The publication provides updates on new acquisitions and exhibitions, and informs readers about new trends and historically significant works of art.

3 NOMA Photography Collection

The museum *(below)* began acquiring photographs in 1973, and now boasts over 7,000 images featuring some of the greatest achievements within the medium. The photography displayed here includes works by Diane Arbus, Henry Fox Talbot, Ansel Adams, Man Ray, and Clarence John Laughlin.

4 Contemporary Art
This display *(above)* covers 20th-century European and American art, encompassing the major movements over the past century. Pieces by Andy Warhol are a highlight.

5 Special Exhibitions
Traveling exhibitions from different parts of the world are displayed here. In the past, NOMA has offered exhibits as diverse as multimedia works by local and international artists to The Treasures of Ancient Egypt.

Key

- First floor
- Second floor
- Third floor

6 Café NOMA
This atmospheric café with floor-to-ceiling windows was opened by restaurant legend Ralph Brennan. The menu features dishes prepared with fresh, seasonal ingredients supplied by local farmers.

7 Wellness Classes in the Sculpture Garden
The Sculpture Garden is an ideal setting for the yoga classes that take place here every Saturday.

8 Where Y'Art
Every Friday at 5pm, NOMA hosts different kinds of special events. These often include visiting exhibitions, film screenings, lectures, hands-on art workshops, family-friendly activities, and live performances.

9 Museum Shop
No trip to NOMA is complete without a visit to the Museum Shop *(below)*. It stocks varied products, such as glass art, prints, books, and jewelry, among other things. The shop ships items worldwide.

The Building

Most visitors to NOMA are as dazzled by the building as they are by its exhibits. The Neo-Classical architecture of the original structure dates back to 1910. It was a gift from sugar broker Isaac Delgado, who envisioned a "temple of art for the rich and poor alike." New wings have been added to the museum, and they complement the original structure, while seamlessly integrating into the surrounding natural environment.

10 Annual Odyssey Ball
Considered to be the premier event on the city's social calendar, the Annual Odyssey Ball takes place every November. On this day, the museum is beautifully decorated and features auctions, a live orchestra, and dancing.

Left **Art of the Americas exhibit** Center **African tribal art** Right **Decorative furniture on display**

Top 10 Further Features of NOMA

1 Louisiana Art
Issac Delagado, a Louisiana sugar broker, founded NOMA. He encouraged the inclusion of local art and today the collection features a vast array of Louisiana art from the 19th and 20th centuries, as well as works by contemporary Louisiana artists.

2 School Programs
A great resource for art educators throughout Louisiana, NOMA offers a variety of educational programs that cover painting, mixed media, and more.

3 African Art
This particular collection is considered one of the most important of its kind in American art museums. It features masks, figures, sculptures, ancient terracottas, textiles, furniture, costumes, marionettes, and musical instruments.

4 European Art
The European section showcases a collection of French, Italian, Dutch, Flemish, and Impressionist works. The highlight is a wealth of timeless Italian paintings from the Renaissance to the 18th century. The French collection includes a series of landscape paintings.

Third Floor

Second Floor

First Floor

The European Art gallery also has works from all the major schools of art over a period of six centuries.

5 Art of the Americas
North, Central, and South American art are the focus here, with works spanning Latin America, Mexico, and the United States. Works displayed range from Mayan artifacts to pre-Columbian artworks, right through to the Spanish-Colonial period. It also includes a Native American collection dating from ancient times to the present day.

6 Oceanic Art
Tribal art from Polynesia, Indonesia, and Melanesia are at the forefront of this collection from the Oceania region. Do not miss the rare pieces from Borneo and the Nias Islands, as well as the fine cotton ritual weavings from Sumatra.

Tribal figure, Oceanic Art

7 Prints and Drawings
This collection includes nearly 7,000 prints, books, and unique works on paper, the majority created by noted 19th- and 20th-century European and American artists. This particular department has two exhibitions a year. Highlights include works by Henri Matisse.

Top 10 Highlights

1. Élisabeth-Louise Vigée Lebrun's portrait of Marie Antoinette, Queen of France

2. William-Adolphe Bouguereau's *Whisperings of Love*

3. Bartolomeo Vivarini's *The Coronation of the Virgin*, a stunning oil painting with a gilded background

4. Edgar Degas' portrait of Estelle Musson

5. Sévres porcelain from the 18th to the early 20th century

6. 8th-century Polynesian temple figure, collected by James Cook on his third voyage to the Hawaiian Islands in 1779

Permanent Exhibits

The permanent collection of the New Orleans Museum of Art includes almost 40,000 artifacts which come from all over the world. Among the highlights are rare pieces from the Americas, Asia, and Europe. The collection continues to grow with new acquisitions. Aficionados will probably notice the preponderance of French and American art.

7. *Death Comes to the Banquet Table* by Giovanni Martinelli

8. Chinese jade and hardstone carvings donated by the Morgan-Whitney family

9. Stern Collection of 19th-century porcelain *veilleuses* (night lights)

10. About 12,000 pieces in the glass collection, from Ancient Egypt to contemporary creations

Whisperings of Love (1885), William-Adolphe Bouguereau

Figurines on display in the Asian Art exhibit

Asian Art

8 NOMA began its collection of Asian art in 1914 with a selection of Chinese jade and stone carvings. Today there are Chinese ceramics, Japanese Edo-period (1603–1838) paintings, and sculptures from India.

Decorative Art

9 More than 15,000 works comprise this distinctive collection, covering glass art, American art pottery, French ceramics, miniature portraits, furniture, and a beautiful representation of the works of Fabergé, which includes 44 miniature Easter eggs.

Cell-Phone Tours

10 The cell-phone tour of the Sydney & Walda Besthoff Sculpture Garden *(see p82)* has become one of the most popular attractions at the museum. This interactive guide is accessible through any phone and is free. The tour focuses on 20 of the sculptures on display.

Pottery, Decorative Art gallery

For more information on museums See pp36–7.

TOP 10 Audubon Zoo

Run by the Audubon Nature Institute, which also maintains the Aquarium of the Americas (see pp18–19), the Insectarium (see p31), and the Audubon Zoo, this world-class facility can trace its history back to the 19th century. Today, covering 58 acres (23 ha) of land, it is regarded among the finest zoos in the country. The Audubon shelters some of the rarest animals in the world and includes an irresistible baby animal nursery, interactive exhibits, and entertaining rides, all amid century-old oaks and lush landscaping.

World of Primates

🚋 The trip to the zoo can be as much fun as the destination itself. Catch a streetcar anywhere along the historic St. Charles Avenue and see the sights as you make your way to the zoo. The ride takes about 30 minutes.

🍴 Stop at the Zoofari Café housed in a historic building from the 1930s to enjoy a burger, hot dog, or chicken wings.

• 6500 Magazine St.
• Map A6
• 504-581-4629
• Open 10am–5pm Tue–Sun
• Adm $13.50 for adults, $8.50 for children under 12, $10.50 for seniors
• www.audubon-institute.org
• St. Charles streetcar

Top 10 Features

1. Louisiana Swamp Exhibit
2. Jaguar Jungle
3. White Tigers
4. Monkey Hill
5. Safari Simulator Ride
6. Red River Hog Exhibit
7. Sea Lions
8. African Savanna Exhibit
9. World of Primates
10. The Dragon's Lair

1 Louisiana Swamp Exhibit

The next best thing to a real Louisiana swamp, this exhibit *(below)* features bears, alligators, raccoons, a baby animal nursery, and a Cajun houseboat. A Swamp Festival is held every November, celebrating the Cajun way of life.

2 Jaguar Jungle

This is an innovative exhibit *(right)* highlighting the ancient Mayan civilization. The display has recreated ruins along with a simulated archaeological dig site in a rain-forest setting. It houses jaguars and spider monkeys, among others.

3 White Tigers

Two of the most memorable inmates of the Audubon Zoo are its pair of playful white tigers. The animals are white with pale-brown and grey stripes, and are called Rex and Zulu after the main Mardi Gras parades.

4 Monkey Hill

Children enjoy climbing this man-made hill *(main image)*, which is the highest point in the city. At the crest are more attractions, including a tree house, rope bridge, and wading pools.

5 Safari Simulator Ride

On this ride *(left)*, seats move in perfect synchronization with wildlife images that are projected on to a large screen, giving viewers a life-like jungle experience.

6 Red River Hog Exhibit

This exhibit comprises two very friendly and tiny African pigs called Matthew and Isabel, who moved to New Orleans from the Denver Zoo.

8 African Savanna Exhibit

This section of the zoo *(above)* is home to the endangered Southern white rhinoceros, which is rapidly declining in its natural habitat. Visitors can also see zebras and ostriches here.

9 World of Primates

This is a very popular exhibit that houses different apes including the endangered species of Sumatran orangutans. The World of Primates showcases, as well as helps to preserve these delightful creatures.

The Dragon's Lair 10

Dragons remain among the most mysterious creatures, and here *(right)* you can get an up-close look at 200-lb (90-kg) Komodo Dragons and more than 100 species of reptiles.

7 Sea Lions

Among the most entertaining animals in the zoo, the sea lions made their debut here in 1928. They have a special routine for guests, and interestingly enough, their habitat *(above)* is a popular wedding location in the city.

A Rich History

Audubon Zoo has existed in various forms for over a century. Originally, animals were exhibited on this site as part of the 1884 World Cotton Exposition *(see p34)*. Many of the zoo's current structures were built by the Works Progress Administration after the Depression in the 1930s. It fell into disrepair in the 1970s and was rebuilt again. Today, this is one of the most well-designed zoos in the country.

☆10 Royal Street

Just around the block from the bustle of Bourbon Street is the picturesque Royal Street, which boasts some of the country's best antique stores, restaurants, and art galleries. Antiques collectors and art-lovers travel from all over the world to shop on this street. Visitors can stay at historic hotels, enjoy leisurely breakfasts at sunny cafés, or indulge in gourmet cuisine at the numerous specialty restaurants. The retailers on Royal Street include European-style boutiques, glass artists, and purveyors of fine collectibles.

The historic Hotel Monteleone

🗘 Do not miss the interesting boutiques tucked away on the little side streets.

• Map L4
• Hotel Monteleone: 214 Royal St.; 504-523-3341
• Brennan's Restaurant: 417 Royal St.; 504-525-9711; $$$$$
• Rodrigue Studio: 730 Royal St.; 504-581-4244; 10am–6pm Mon–Sat; noon–5pm Sun
• Louisiana Supreme Court: 400 Royal St.; 504-310-2300
• Fleur de Paris: 523 Royal St.; 504-525-1899
• Mr. B's Bistro: 201 Royal St.; 504-523-2078; $$$$$
• Cornstalk Hotel: 915 Royal St.; 504-523-1515 www.cornstalkhotel.com
• Court of Two Sisters: 613 Royal St.; 504-522-7261
• Gallier House Museum: 1132 Royal St.; 504-525-5661; call for timings; adm $10 for adults, $8 for children and seniors; www.hgghh.org
• Omni Royal Orleans Hotel: 621 St. Louis St.; 504-529–5333

Top 10 Features

1. Hotel Monteleone
2. Brennan's Restaurant
3. Rodrigue Studio
4. Louisiana Supreme Court
5. Fleur de Paris
6. Mr. B's Bistro
7. Cornstalk Hotel
8. Court of Two Sisters
9. Gallier House Museum
10. Omni Royal Orleans Hotel

Hotel Monteleone
Despite rumors of being haunted, this exquisite hotel remains the *grande dame* of the city. After a multi-million dollar makeover, the property is as stunning as its contemporary counterparts.

Rodrigue Studio
The world-renowned "Blue Dog" paintings were created here *(above)* by Louisiana artist George Rodrigue. Today, his typically Southern art is highly coveted and valued.

Louisiana Supreme Court
A massive face-lift has restored this huge stone and marble structure *(right)* to its former glory. The Beaux Arts-style building dates back to 1910 and represents the city's architectural heritage.

Brennan's Restaurant
The only place in the city with a suggested wine for each breakfast *entrée*, this Creole restaurant is famous for inventing the deliciously sinful bananas foster (flambéed bananas with ice cream).

For restaurant price categories **See p71.**

Fleur de Paris

The only boutique of its kind in the South, this lovely shop *(left)* boasts couture clothing as well as stunning hats for women, all designed and created at the store itself.

Mr. B's Bistro

Located at the corner of Royal and Iberville Streets, this restaurant's chief draw is its Creole cuisine. Mr. B's signature dish is the "Gumbo Ya-Ya" (gumbo with pork sausage and chicken).

Cornstalk Hotel

Aptly named because of the cornstalk design on the iron fence encircling the building, this hotel *(above)* has the old-world charm of a fine bed and breakfast.

Court of Two Sisters

This historic restaurant was originally a shop owned by two Creole sisters who sold sewing accessories. Today, it is owned by two brothers but still retains its original name, and is famous for its daily buffet accompanied by live Dixieland jazz.

Gallier House Museum

Designed by James Gallier Jr., this grand 19th-century mansion *(right)* is an amalgam of Creole and American styles. It also inspired author Anne Rice to create Louis and Lestat's home in *Interview with the Vampire*.

Omni Royal Orleans Hotel

Considered one of the area's premier properties, this hotel was built on the site of the 1836 St. Louis Hotel. It has a rooftop pool, and houses the Rib Room, one of the city's finest restaurants.

Upscale Dining on Royal Street

It is only fitting that some of the best fine-dining spots in the city are on this magnificent French Quarter street. A good day on Royal Street would include breakfast at Brenann's Restaurant, lunch at the Rib Room, and dinner at Mr. B's Bistro. In between, plan a leisurely cocktail hour at the stylish bar at Omni Royal Orleans Hotel.

Left **M.S. Rau Antiques** Center **Items at The Brass Monkey** Right **James H. Cohen & Sons, Inc.**

🔟 Shopping for Antiques

1 M.S. Rau Antiques

This store has been around for over a century. Its 25,000-sq-ft (2,300-sq-m) space is stocked with beautiful jewelry, 18th- and 19th-century fine art, and *objets d'art*. M.S. Rau is also famous for its impressive range of American, French, and English antique furniture. ⬥ *630 Royal St.* • *Map M4* • *504-523-5660*

2 Harris Antiques

Harris has one of the largest selections of 18th-, 19th-, and early 20th-century French, Italian, and English furniture, grandfather clocks, and French mantle clocks, as well as one of the best collections of antique bronzes and marble sculptures in the South. ⬥ *233 Royal St.* • *Map M3* • *504-523-1605*

3 French Antique Shop

For more than six decades, this family-owned store has offered a great collection of antique chandeliers and lamps. The French Antique Shop also stocks fine art, furniture, tapestries, and much more. Located in the second block of Royal Street, this is the perfect place to begin shopping. ⬥ *225 Royal St.* • *Map M3* • *504-524-9861*

4 Ida Manheim Antiques

This famous gallery was originally a small cabinet shop. Today, this family-owned store has a fine selection of English, Continental, and Oriental furnishings, porcelains, jade, silver, and paintings. ⬥ *409 Royal St.* • *Map M4* • *504-620-4114*

5 Royal Antiques

Boasting some of the most elegant pieces in the French Quarter, this store's collection includes lovely French mirrors, Biedermeier furniture, and Chippendale chairs *(see p99)*.

6 Keil's Antiques

Operating since 1899, the three-story Keil's Antiques offers thousands of French and English antiques, including jewelry, chandeliers, furniture, and table-top items. The proprietors of Keil's also own Moss Antiques and Royal Antiques on the same street. The best thing about this store is that there is something for every kind of budget. ⬥ *325 Royal St.* • *Map M4* • *504-522-4552*

Chandeliers and *objets d'art* in the French Antique Shop

Top 10 Unique Galleries on Royal Street

Art Shopping on Royal Street

The art scene in New Orleans is a vibrant and integral part of the city's culture and economy. Galleries flourish in virtually every nook of the city, showcasing works by artists ranging from fresh local talent to renowned names. New trends and styles have developed out of the city's eclectic culture and New Orleans is considered to be the new hub of art. Serious collectors travel across the world to catch the latest showings. On the first Saturday night of each month, galleries throughout the city hold a wine and cheese open house, where they welcome all visitors to view their collections.

Paintings by Joachim Casell and other New Orleans artists, Casell Gallery

Waldhorn & Adler

7 One of the oldest antique stores in the South, Waldhorn & Adler specializes in 18th- and 19th-century furniture and antique and estate jewelry. The store is housed in a restored building built in 1800 by Edgar Degas' great-grandfather. ✆ 343 Royal St. • Map M4 • 504-581-6379 • Closed Sun–Mon

Moss Antiques

8 This store specializes in silver, period jewelry, wooden boxes, Limoges enamel, antique furnishings and chandeliers. Their selection of art and sculpture is also noteworthy *(see p99)*.

James H. Cohen & Sons, Inc.

9 Established in 1898, this is the only shop in New Orleans that specializes in rare coins and currency, antique firearms, swords, and unusual collectibles such as old ballot boxes and World War I telescopes. ✆ 437 Royal St. • Map M4 • 504-522-3305

The Brass Monkey

10 This store has the largest collection of Limoges boxes in the city and caters to an eclectic taste. The inventory includes antique walking sticks, Venetian glass, and medical instruments *(see p99)*.

For more on shopping See pp40–41.

🔟 Aquarium of the Americas

An impressive attraction offering vistors the chance to see a walk-through underwater tunnel, a gallery of seahorses, a white alligator, baby sharks, and a stunning rain forest under one roof, this is one of the premier tourist destinations in the city. Showcasing nearly 500 species of aquatic life, this aquarium is one of the biggest in the country. Although most of the fish died due to a massive generator failure after Hurricane Katrina, other inmates were saved and brought back when the Aquarium reopened in 2006.

Adventure Island

⊘ A trip to the aquarium, along with a stroll through the nearby Riverwalk Marketplace along the Mississippi River, can be a day-long excursion. Take a journey down the river on a quaint paddlewheel steamboat.

⊖ The aquarium's food court offers basic fast food. No food or drinks are allowed to be brought in from outside. Within walking distance are some small cafés, great for coffee, snacks, or lunch.

• 1 Canal Street
• Map N5
• 504-581-4629
• 10am–5pm Tue–Sun
• Adm $18.50 for adults; $11.50 for children under 12; $14.50 for seniors
• www.audubon-institute.org
• Riverfront streetcar

Top 10 Features

1 Frogs!
2 Adventure Island
3 Amazon Rain Forest
4 Living in Water Gallery
5 Seahorse Gallery
6 The Gulf of Mexico Exhibit
7 Mississippi River Gallery
8 Caribbean Reef Exhibit
9 Penguin Gallery
10 Aquarium Scavenger Hunt

Frogs!
This display *(above)* has milk frogs, poison dart frogs, and other amphibians living amid beautiful plants. There are also neon colored frogs which can be seen hopping around in the dark.

Adventure Island
This wonderland of interactive exhibits offers children a fun way of learning about aquatic life. Highlights are the pirate ship and stingrays, which can be fed.

Amazon Rain Forest
This superb re-creation of the Amazon rain forest *(below)* is a fascinating version of the real thing. Exotic orchids grow here, while piranhas lurk in the flowing waters below the thick forest canopy, inhabited by colorful tropical birds.

4 Living in Water Gallery

This gallery focuses on the adaptations and behavior patterns required to survive in the water. This gallery is the only permanent exhibit that includes animals which are not indigenous to the Americas.

5 Seahorse Gallery

This section *(above)* acquaints people with varied and wonderful species of seahorses, many of which are endangered. The aquarium's Project Seahorse is working towards the conservation of the species.

6 The Gulf of Mexico Exhibit

Sharks, groupers, redfish, and a giant sea turtle named King Mydas live harmoniously in the Gulf of Mexico exhibit, which contains a replica of an offshore oil rig. Visitors can learn how these marine creatures deal with human intervention, as well as how multiple species can peacefully co-exist.

7 Mississippi River Gallery

This gallery *(right)* offers a ringside view of the Mississippi's inhabitants. Do not miss one of the most compelling sights here – a blue-eyed white alligator called Spots. Also watch out for the catfish, the sunfish, and gar.

8 Caribbean Reef Exhibit

One of the most exciting parts of the aquarium, the Caribbean Reef Exhibit *(main image)* is a walk-through aquatic tunnel which is 30 ft (9 m) long and surrounded by 132,000 gallons (5,00,000 liters) of water. From here, visitors will get one of the best views of marine life in the country.

9 Penguin Gallery

These birds *(right)* are a delightful sight and a good time to view them is during the daily feedings, at 10:30am and 3pm. Do not be surprised at the lack of snow – these penguins are from a temperate zone.

10 Aquarium Scavenger Hunt

Those visiting the aquarium in large groups can enjoy a scavenger hunt, which is both exciting and informative. Instructions can be downloaded from the aquarium's website.

Parakeet Pointe

Located within the aquarium is Parakeet Pointe, which is an 800 sq ft (244 sq m) outdoor environment that is home to hundreds of colorful parakeets. This delightful avian habitat offers visitors an interactive experience where they can purchase seed sticks, for a small sum, and feed the birds as they stroll through the free-flight exhibit.

⁙⁙⁙⁙ Mississippi Riverfront

Over the years there has been a stunning redevelopment of the Mississippi Riverfront. New businesses, attractions, and special events have made this area a must-see for any visitor to New Orleans. A streetcar line runs the length of the Riverfront, with stops at all of the popular sites. The riverfront is within walking distance of the Warehouse District, the CBD, and many of the best hotels and restaurants. The long pedestrian path along the riverfront is called the Moonwalk, and is perfect for a romantic stroll.

JAX Brewery

🍹 The best selection of refreshments can be found inside the Riverwalk Marketplace.

• Map N5
• JAX Brewery: 600 Decatur St.; 504-566-7245; open 10am–7pm daily; www.jackson-brewery.com
• Creole Queen: 1 Poydras St.; 504-529-4567; cruises 2–3:30pm Fri–Sat; adm $20 for adults, $10 for children under 12; www.creolequeen.com
• The Crazy Lobster Bar and Grill: 1 Poydras St.; 504-569-3380; $ (for price categories see p71)
• Riverwalk Marketplace: 1 Poydras St.; 504-522-1555
• Ernest P. Morial Convention Center: 900 Convention Center Blvd; www.mccno.com
• Entergy IMAX Theatre: 1 Canal St.; 504-581-4629; call for timings; adm $9.95 for adults, $6.95 for children under 12, $8.95 for seniors; www.auduboninstitute.org

Top 10 Features

1. Woldenberg Riverfront Park
2. JAX Brewery
3. Moonwalk
4. Creole Queen
5. Riverwalk Marketplace
6. The Crazy Lobster Bar and Grill
7. Spanish Plaza
8. Ernest P. Morial Convention Center
9. Entergy IMAX Theatre
10. Riverfront Streetcar

1 Woldenberg Riverfront Park

This green space *(below)* is one of the most peaceful spots in the downtown area. The park also hosts events, concerts, and festivals throughout the year.

2 JAX Brewery

Once a working brewery, today, the renovated JAX building houses unique shops, boutiques, and restaurants right by the river. It also has a museum that traces the brewery's history.

3 Moonwalk

Running the length of the riverfront, the Moonwalk *(main image)* is a heavily traveled walkway. There are benches along the way where visitors can relax and watch the river.

4 Creole Queen

The best way to experience the river is on a 2-hour dinner cruise on the Creole Queen *(below)*, an authentic paddlewheel steamboat.

Riverwalk Marketplace
This indoor complex *(above)* is two blocks long and faces the Mississippi River. Shop at a variety of retailers and enjoy some of the best local delicacies here.

The Crazy Lobster Bar and Grill
Indulge in the house specialty – a large bucket of steamed seafood, or try a giant lobster grilled to perfection along with an icy beer. To top off the perfect meal, sit outdoors, right by the river, and enjoy the live jazz.

Spanish Plaza
Located between Riverwalk Marketplace and the Aquarium of the Americas *(see pp18–19)*, the Spanish Plaza is a huge common area, the site of year-round special events and concerts.

Entergy IMAX Theatre
Equipped with a large screen and outstanding sound system, the IMAX Theatre *(above)* offers a spectacular viewing experience.

Ernest P. Morial Convention Center
This is the largest convention-center space on a single level in the country. It hosts some of the biggest and most prestigious conventions in the world. The center also features state-of-the-art technology.

Riverfront Streetcar
The bright-red Mississippi Riverfront streetcars *(right)* are the newest addition to the city's traditional transit system. The streetcar stops intermittently along the riverfront at all the major shopping and tourist attractions.

Getting Around the Riverfront
The riverfront is a vital part of the downtown area. Just across from the JAX Brewery, there is a ticketing kiosk where visitors can purchase tickets for river cruises (including dinner cruises). Transportation in and around the riverfront is frequent and convenient. The streetcar stops near the aquarium and runs until 10:30pm daily, while the ferry from downtown to the West Bank of New Orleans runs till just after midnight.

Mardi Gras

New Orleans bills its annual Mardi Gras celebration as "the biggest street party in the world." More than a million visitors from around the world gather in the city up to three weeks before the festival. Lavish parades are staged by various Mardi Gras clubs, known as "krewes," along with parties and street gatherings. New Orleans is the place to be during this time to let your hair down, don an outrageous costume, eat great food, vie for beads thrown from parade floats, and generally party hard for the last time before Lent.

Mardi Gras float on St. Charles Avenue

🕐 The crowd is usually well-behaved, but be careful of your purses, wallets, and other personal items. Stay on streets that are highly populated. Be warned that a lot of alcohol is consumed during Mardi Gras, so try to steer clear of drunken revelers.

🍴 Bars are open citywide during Mardi Gras, although food is a different story. Either bring your own or try the snacks available from street vendors. On St. Charles Avenue, people generally bring their own coolers and snacks.

• Mardi Gras is celebrated on the Tuesday before Lent but celebrations begin as early as 6th January with the night of Epiphany (the festival marking the revelation of God as Jesus Christ).

Top 10 Features

1. Lundi Gras on Spanish Plaza
2. Krewe of Barkus Dog Parade
3. Bourbon Street Awards Costume Contest
4. Krewe of Armenius Gay Mardi Gras Ball
5. Krewe of Rex Parade
6. Krewe of Zulu Parade
7. Krewe of Endymion Parade
8. Krewe of Bacchus Parade
9. Krewe du Vieux
10. Mardi Gras on St. Charles Avenue

1 Lundi Gras on Spanish Plaza

Rex, the King of Carnival, arrives auspiciously on the Mississippi River on Lundi Gras, which is the day before Mardi Gras. His arrival is heralded with fireworks and a party that continues in the Woldenberg Riverfront Park.

2 Krewe of Barkus Dog Parade

Every year, dog owners dress themselves and their pets in matching costumes and parade through the French Quarter *(below)*. Themes for the dog parade include a "Streetbark Named Desire" and "Tail House Rock."

3 Bourbon Street Awards Costume Contest

This costume contest *(above)* held on Mardi Gras afternoon, showcases some of the most outrageous and imaginative costumes of the festival. Staged on Bourbon Street, it attracts thousands of locals and visitors alike.

4 Krewe of Armenius Gay Mardi Gras Ball
The gay community produces some of the most elaborate Mardi Gras balls. The Krewe of Armenius throws balls which are camp and uproariously funny. Their costumes are also among the best in the city.

5 Krewe of Rex Parade
The crown jewel of Mardi Gras is the Krewe of Rex Parade *(main image)*. Rex has reigned as King of the Carnival since he first appeared in 1872, and has since defined the festival with the royal colors of purple, green, and gold.

6 Krewe of Zulu Parade
Just before the Rex Parade is the Krewe of Zulu *(above)* on the morning of Mardi Gras. The Zulu Social Aid and Pleasure Club produces one of the most festive parades, inspired by one of Africa's fiercest tribes.

7 Krewe of Endymion Parade
Considered one of the longest and most elaborate parades, Endymion rolls out on the Saturday before Mardi Gras. The Endymion ball is one of the most popular in town and continues all night.

9 Krewe du Vieux
If it can be mocked, the Krewe du Vieux will mock it in their highly anticipated parade *(above)*. Typical themes of this walking-only parade group are satirical and bawdy.

8 Krewe of Bacchus Parade
The Bacchus Parade *(below)* on the Sunday before Mardi Gras features some of the largest and longest floats including the King Kong, the Queen Kong, and the heralded Bachagator.

Blaine Kern's Mardi Gras World
Blaine Kern is the master Mardi Gras float designer and builder in New Orleans and his Mardi Gras World is a year-round facility open to the public. Here, visitors can see how the props and floats are conceived, designed, and constructed. Giant character heads and floats from past Mardi Gras festivals are displayed in this building. The space is also rented out for private parties and receptions *(see p56)*.

10 Mardi Gras on St. Charles Avenue
On Mardi Gras, groups of friends and families stake out their territory along the historic St. Charles Avenue to watch the Rex and Zulu parades, as well as the "everyman" truck parades that follow them.

10 Jackson Square

The elegant centerpiece of the French Quarter, Jackson Square is an attractive and lively meeting place. Known as the "Place d'Armes" in the 18th century, it was later renamed in honor of the Battle of New Orleans hero, Andrew Jackson. An imposing statue of Jackson dominates the square, with the St. Louis Cathedral providing a majestic backdrop. Quaint shops line the perimeter of the park, and local artists, mimes, palm and tarot-card readers, and musicians sell their wares and perform here everyday.

Entrance to the Place d'Armes Hotel

🚕 Enjoy a romantic evening on a mule-drawn buggy around the Square.

☕ Try the famous coffee and *beignets (see p54),* a New Orleans' favourite, at the Café du Monde.

• Map M5
• St. Louis Cathedral: 615 Pere Antoine Alley; 504-525-9585; tours: 1–4pm Wed–Sat; www.stlouiscathedral.org
• Pontalba Apartment Buildings: St. Peter and St. Ann Sts.
• The Cabildo and The Presbytère: Jackson Square; 504-568-6968; open 9am–5pm Tue–Sun; adm $6
• Place d'Armes Hotel: 625 St. Ann St.; 504-524-4531; www.placedarmes.com; $$$ (for price categories see p115)
• Faulkner House Books: 624 Pirate's Alley; 504-524-2940; www.faulknerhousebooks.net

Top 10 Features
1 St. Louis Cathedral
2 Pontalba Apartment Buildings
3 Pedestrian Walkway
4 The Cabildo
5 Place d'Armes Hotel
6 Faulkner House Books
7 Andrew Jackson Statue
8 Artistic Community
9 The Presbytère
10 Street Musicians

St. Louis Cathedral
This is the oldest continuously active Catholic church in the country *(right),* first built in 1727, and rebuilt twice since then. Dramatic lighting makes even the back of the church look imposing.

Pontalba Apartment Buildings
Built in the mid-19th century, these are the oldest apartments *(below)* in the country. These buildings are among the most enviable addresses in the city.

Pedestrian Walkway
Jackson Square's perimeter is lined with stores and boutiques. Pedestrians can spend hours strolling among the musicians, jesters, and artists who work here.

The Cabildo
The site of the 1803 Louisiana Purchase *(see p34)* and one of the buildings comprising the Louisiana State Museum, the Cabildo features more than 1,000 artifacts, original art pieces, and rotating exhibits highlighting local history.

Place d'Armes Hotel
Conveniently located on the edge of Jackson Square, the Place d'Armes Hotel is a charming place close to most of the attractions of the French Quarter. The exquisitely restored 18th- and 19th-century buildings surround a lovely courtyard.

6 Faulkner House Books
This two-story building *(above)* was once home to author William Faulkner. Today, it is a National Historic Landmark and houses one of the finest bookstores in the city.

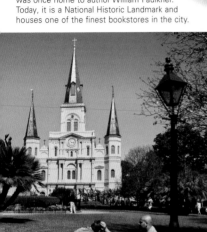

7 Andrew Jackson Statue
Commander of the American forces at the Battle of New Orleans and the 7th president of the U.S., Andrew Jackson is commemorated throughout the city. An extremely elegant memorial is his bronze statue *(above)* in the middle of Jackson Square.

8 Artistic Community
New Orleans artists do not always need a studio to create fine works of art. Many of them work and sell their creations in and around Jackson Square itself.

9 The Presbytère
This circa-1791 building is part of the Louisiana State Museum. The Presbytère houses a fantastic Mardi Gras exhibit *(above)*, as well as some of the finest ball gowns and costumes from past Mardi Gras celebrations. It also has a fabulous gift shop.

10 Street Musicians
New Orleans is best known for its food and music. The grassroots musicians *(right)*, who make their living playing on the streets, are most at home in the heart of Jackson Square.

Jackson Square in the Movies
If Jackson Square looks familiar even on a first visit, it may be because it has been used as a backdrop in several movies. The Square was a featured location in *The Curious Case of Benjamin Button* (2008). In the past, it has been used in other motion pictures, television programs, and music videos. The New Orleans Office of Film and Video fields frequent requests for the use of Jackson Square as a location for major Hollywood productions.

🔟 New Orleans City Park

Built on the site of the former Allard Plantation beside the Bayou St. John, the New Orleans City Park is one of the biggest urban parks in the country, covering an area of 1,300 acres (518 ha). A perfect spot for children and adults alike, it offers sports facilities, museums, waterways, golf courses, an amusement park, botanical gardens, and much more. The park is also home to the New Orleans Museum of Art and the Sydney & Walda Besthoff Sculpture Garden, which showcases over 50 modern sculptures.

Giant oak tree at New Orleans City Park

🕖 The park may seem overwhelming to first-time visitors. Visit the website to download a map and guide to the park.

🍴 The Parkview Café is a good place to relax your tired feet. It offers burgers and cold drinks.

- 1 Palm Drive
- Map H1
- 504-482-4888
- www.neworleans-citypark.com
- St. Charles streetcar
- New Orleans Botanical Gardens: 10am–4:30pm Tue–Sat, noon–5pm Sun; adm $6 for adults, $3 for children
- Storyland: 504-482-4888; open 10am–3pm Tue–Fri, 11am–6pm Sat–Sun; adm $3
- Carousel Gardens Amusement Park: 11am–6pm Sat–Sun; adm $3
- Train Garden: 10am–4:30pm Tue–Sun; trains run on weekends; adm $6 for adults, $3 for children

Top 10 Features

1. New Orleans Botanical Gardens
2. Storyland
3. City Park Golf Course
4. Pepsi Tennis Center
5. Old Oak Grove
6. Celebration in the Oaks
7. New Orleans Museum of Art
8. Pavilion of Two Sisters
9. Carousel Gardens Amusement Park
10. The Train Garden

New Orleans Botanical Gardens
Botanical exhibits, themed gardens – including the famous rose gardens – cover 10 acres (4 ha) of this park *(main image)*. Statues by artist Enrique Alférez stand among the trees here.

Storyland
This fairytale playground *(above)*, with more than 25 exhibits from storybooks, is a major attraction for families. It is an ideal setting for children's parties.

City Park Golf Course
The old golf course at the City Park was redesigned to include an 18-hole facility *(right)*, 74 driving-range stalls and two grass hitting areas.

Pepsi Tennis Center
With 16 hard and 10 clay courts, this facility offers the best public tennis courts in the state of Louisiana. Visitors can rent equipment, but it is best to book in advance.

Old Oak Grove
New Orleans is home to the largest grove of mature oaks in the country. The oldest tree in this majestic collection is believed to be over 800 years old.

Celebration in the Oaks
The park is adorned with magnificent themed decorations and state-of-the-art lighting during the holiday season, from Thanksgiving to New Year's Day. This is a favorite stop on most walking and driving tours.

New Orleans Museum of Art
The museum *(above)* is the centerpiece of City Park, with magnificent permanent collections, as well as an adjacent outdoor sculpture garden, and rotating, visiting exhibitions *(see pp8–11)*.

Pavilion of Two Sisters
The semi-circular pavilion *(right)* is built in the style of a European orangery and has become a popular venue for receptions, fundraisers, and other events.

Carousel Gardens Amusement Park
With one of the last 100 antique carousels in the country, this ride *(right)* is the main attraction of this charming amusement park. It also includes a dozen other rides which make the place a children's wonderland.

The Train Garden
One of the most unique attractions in the park is a working miniature-train garden, elevated to eye level, with authentic re-creations of the historic architectural structures of New Orleans.

City Bark
Dog lovers visit City Park all the time, so the park officials created an entire section just for canines called "City Bark." It has separate facilities for large and small dogs, and those who bring their animals here must subscribe to the annual membership. The park is dotted with wooded trails, shaded areas, flowering trees, and even a dog wash for messy animals.

🔟 Bourbon Street

This iconic French Quarter street never sleeps. It dates back to 1718, when it was known as Rue Bourbon, and still retains some of the original 18th-century architecture, which can be seen on a leisurely walk down the length of the street. With around-the-clock live music, parties, all-night bars and clubs, Bourbon Street's atmosphere of revelry is unmatched in the city. Renowned restaurants lie interspersed between unique shops and vendors. Every visitor to New Orleans should experience life on Bourbon Street.

Galatoire's restaurant

🔗 It is legal to carry alcohol on Bourbon Street. All the bars have "to go" cups.

- Map M3
- Chris Owens Club: 500 Bourbon St.; 504-523-6400
- Lafitte's Blacksmith Shop: 941 Bourbon St.; 504-593-9761
- Famous Door: 339 Bourbon St.; 504-598-4334
- Pat O'Brien's Bar: 718 St. Peter St.; 504-525-4823
- Galatoire's Restaurant: 209 Bourbon St.; 504-525-2021; closed Mon; $$$$$ (for price categories see p71)
- Royal Sonesta Hotel: 300 Bourbon St.; 504-586-0300; www.royalsonesta.com; $$$$$ (for price categories see p115)
- Preservation Hall: 726 St. Peter Street; 504-522-2841
- Cat's Meow Karaoke Club: 701 Bourbon St.; 504-523-2788
- Bourbon House Restaurant: 144 Bourbon St.; 504-522-0111; $$$$ (for price categories see p71)

Top 10 Features

1. Chris Owens Club
2. Lafitte's Blacksmith Shop
3. Famous Door
4. Pat O'Brien's Bar
5. Galatoire's Restaurant
6. Royal Sonesta Hotel
7. Preservation Hall
8. Gay and Lesbian Entertainment
9. Cat's Meow Karaoke Club
10. Bourbon House Restaurant

1 Chris Owens Club

The eternally youthful entertainer Chris Owens takes to the stage six nights a week at her club on Bourbon Street. For decades now, Owens has been providing her patrons with a Las Vegas-style variety show that never gets dated.

2 Lafitte's Blacksmith Shop

This late-18th-century Creole cottage *(above)* may look decrepit, but it houses one of the French Quarter's nicest watering holes. This is one of the best spots for people-watching in the area.

3 Famous Door

This loud and raucous club *(right)* is packed every night. The Famous Door is a typical all-night Bourbon Street nightclub.

4 Pat O'Brien's Bar

The infamous rum cocktail, the "Hurricane," was invented here during World War II. Today, this bar still holds its own with a lively ambience and is usually packed.

5 Galatoire's Restaurant

One of the best dining spots in the city, Galatoire's has an old-world charm and fantastic cuisine. The soufflé potatoes are a must-try.

6 Royal Sonesta Hotel

One of the best hotels in the area, the Royal Sonesta *(left)* is on a busy corner of Bourbon Street. Enjoy oysters at The Desire Bar, and the fantastic Irvin Mayfield's Jazz Playhouse.

7 Preservation Hall

New Orleans jazz echoes through this legendary music hall *(above)*. Veteran jazz musicians and new acts still play here weekly.

8 Gay and Lesbian Entertainment

A good portion of Bourbon Street is home to restaurants and bars that cater to the city's sizeable gay and lesbian community. Anchoring the district is the lively Bourbon Pub.

9 Cat's Meow Karaoke Club

With one of the most in-demand stages in the French Quarter, and doors that open right on to the street, Cat's Meow *(right)* has pulsating karaoke music which permeates right through the whole block.

10 Bourbon House Restaurant

Old New Orleans charm blends seamlessly with a contemporary vibe in this Creole eatery *(left)*, in the first block of Bourbon Street. Ask for the special Bourbon House Restaurant frozen-bourbon milk punch.

Living on Bourbon Street

Although internationally known for its unique nightlife and rich history, Bourbon Street is also home for many New Orleanians. The Historic Bourbon Street Foundation sponsors a "Treasures of Bourbon Street" tour every October. This features centuries-old Creole town houses, cottages, and original period architecture. Surprisingly, many of the facades of the street-facing houses are actually the backs of the homes, built to face lush interior courtyards.

🔟 Canal Street

Thought to be the widest street in America, the 170-ft (50-m) wide Canal Street lies in the heart of downtown New Orleans. It runs across the city, from the Mississippi to Lake Pontchartrain. The main activity is around the CBD, where luxury hotels, upscale restaurants, and unique retail establishments line both sides of the street. The Canal streetcar line runs down the middle of the thoroughfare, providing access to Mid-City and the cemeteries.

The World Trade Center

🟢 Cross Canal Street at designated cross walks only.

- Map D3
- Shops at Canal Place: 333 Canal St.; 504-522-9200
- Harrah's New Orleans Casino: 8 Canal St.; 504-533-6000; www. harrahsneworleans.com
- The World Trade Center: 2 Canal St.; 504-529-1601
- The Ritz-Carlton, New Orleans: 921 Canal St.; 504-524-1331; $$$$$ (for price categories see p115)
- The Roosevelt New Orleans: 123 Baronne St.; 504-648-1200; $$$$$
- Rubensteins: 102 St. Charles Ave.; 504-581-6666
- Audubon Insectarium: 423 Canal St.; 504-410-2847; open 10am–5pm Tue–Sun; adm $15.95 for adults, $10.95 for children, $12.95 for seniors; www.audubon-institute.org
- Palace Café: 605 Canal St.; 504-523-1661; $$$$ (for price categories see p71)

Top 10 Features

1. Shops at Canal Place
2. Harrah's New Orleans Casino
3. The World Trade Center
4. The Ritz-Carlton, New Orleans
5. The Roosevelt New Orleans Hotel
6. Cemeteries at Canal Street
7. Rubensteins
8. Audubon Insectarium
9. Canal Street Ferry Line
10. Palace Café

Shops at Canal Place
This complex of offices, stores, restaurants, and theaters *(above)* is right by the Mississippi. The mall is dominated by the upscale Saks Fifth Avenue.

Harrah's New Orleans Casino
Just across from Canal Place, this is the only land-based casino in the city (the other two are on boats). The property *(below)* includes games, a luxurious hotel, fine restaurants, and an ice bar.

The World Trade Center
An imposing skyscraper, the World Trade Center is built right on the banks of the Mississippi. The center was developed to increase international trade and commerce in Louisiana.

The Ritz-Carlton, New Orleans
A historic structure that once housed a department store, this building has been elegantly refashioned into the Ritz-Carlton Hotel. The hotel boasts 450 guest rooms and is home to a world-class spa, a stylish restaurant, M Bistro, and nightly live jazz.

The Roosevelt New Orleans

5 This century-old hotel *(above)* used to be a Fairmont property and is now part of the Waldorf-Astoria hotel group. The hotel features the historic Sazerac Bar and the legendary Blue Room, which still offers live entertainment.

Cemeteries at Canal Street

6 First-time visitors to New Orleans are often surprised that the dead are buried above ground in crypts, rather than below. This is because New Orleans is below sea level. The ornate cemeteries *(above)* at Canal Street are a unique sight to behold.

Rubensteins

7 The city's oldest house of fine fashion, Rubensteins stands at the corner of Canal Street and St. Charles Avenue. This menswear store has been providing quality fabrics and tailoring for New Orleanians since 1924.

Audubon Insectarium

8 Located in the old U.S. Customs House, the Audubon Insectarium offers up-close insect encounters, insect cuisine, an "immersion theater" featuring an animated insect movie, and a chance to "shrink" yourself to insect size.

Canal Street Ferry Line

9 Commuters traveling from the East Bank of New Orleans to the West Bank often use the ferry line at the foot of Canal Street. Passengers can also drive their cars onto the ferry. It is a good way to experience the sights along the river.

Palace Café

10 The elegant early-20th-century building that served as the Werlein's Piano Store for decades, is now the three-story Palace Café *(left)*, which serves contemporary and delicious Creole cuisine. Do not miss the crabmeat cheesecake and white chocolate bread pudding.

Canal Streetcar

For those who truly want to take in the sights of the city at a leisurely pace, the Canal streetcar is the best option. The journey might be a bit slow, but it remains the best way to see the architecture and layout of the city, all the way from the Mississippi to the old and historic cemeteries in the Mid-City area. Tickets for the streetcar cost just $1.25.

Left **Jean Baptiste Le Moyne** Center **Louisiana Superdome** Right **Sketch of St. Louis Cathedral**

TOP 10 Moments in History

1 Founding of New Orleans (1718)

Jean Baptiste Le Moyne de Bienville of the French Mississippi Company founded a colony on the Lower Mississippi and named it "La Nouvelle Orléans." Situated on a curve of the Mississippi River, the site was thought to be immune to floods and hurricanes. Surrounded by the river, lakes and swamps, it also became known as the Isle d'Orleans.

2 New Orleans becomes a Spanish Colony (1763)

New Orleans was ceded to the Spanish in 1763 by Louis XV. However, the French settlers rebelled and forced governor Antonio de Ulloa to abdicate. It was General Alexander O'Reilly who established Spanish control in 1768. Thereafter, the Spanish encouraged trade and turned the city into a commercial center.

3 The Great French Quarter Fire (1788)

Of 1,100 buildings in New Orleans in 1788, 856 were destroyed by a fire on Good Friday. The city only had two fire vehicles, and both were destroyed. After the fire, the city was rebuilt with Spanish-style architecture.

4 Construction of the St. Louis Cathedral (1794)

Although the original St. Louis Church was destroyed by the fire of 1788, by the following year the cornerstone of the new St. Louis Cathedral was in place. This was the third Roman Catholic church to be built on this site since 1718, but the first to be elevated to cathedral status.

Lithograph of the first Mardi Gras parade

5 First Mardi Gras Celebrated (1827)

During Spanish rule, pre-Lent festivals were banned. By 1823, New Orleans had been under U.S. rule for 20 years (the U.S. bought Louisiana from the French through the Louisiana Purchase of 1803), and around 1827, the people were finally permitted to wear masks and celebrate. The first proper Mardi Gras parade was held 10 years later.

6 World Cotton Exposition (1884)

The 1884 World Cotton Exposition lasted six months. Up to a third of all cotton produced in the U.S. was handled in New Orleans, home of the Cotton Exchange. However, despite its scale, this fair was a financial disaster riddled with debt and corruption, especially as treasurer Edward A. Burke stole much of its budget.

Preceding pages **Colorful Mardi Gras floats**

7 New Orleans Football Franchise Awarded (1966)

On All Saints Day in 1966, the National Football League awarded New Orleans the league's 16th major team franchise. The aptly named Saints adopted a gold *fleur de lis* as their team symbol, representing the French colonists who had settled in Louisiana.

8 Construction of the Louisiana Superdome (1975)

It took four years and $163 million to build the huge Louisiana (now Mercedes-Benz) Superdome. The result is an architecturally stunning facility (see p74).

9 Louisiana World Exposition (1984)

The centerpiece of this event was a gondola lift that ferried millions of visitors across the Mississippi River. The fair was the precursor to a major redevelopment of the city's riverfront area.

10 Hurricane Katrina (2005)

The largest disaster in the U.S., Hurricane Katrina hit New Orleans on August 29, 2005. The failing of the city's levees caused massive flooding and destruction, from which the city is still recovering.

Flooded New Orleans after Hurricane Katrina

Top 10 New Orleans Figures

1 Marie Laveau (1801–81)
Known as New Orleans' "Voodoo Queen," Laveau practiced the religion that originated in West Africa.

2 Louis Armstrong (1901–71)
Also known as "Satchmo," Armstrong is globally remembered as a premier jazz trumpeter and singer.

3 Mahalia Jackson (1911–72)
Long heralded as the "Queen of Gospel Music," Jackson has recorded 35 albums.

4 Tennessee Williams (1911–83)
Playwright Williams captured the angst of the American South in his works, including *The Glass Menagerie*.

5 Truman Capote (1924–84)
During his controversial career, Capote authored some of the best-selling novels of his time, including *In Cold Blood*.

6 Stephen Ambrose (1936–2002)
Historian Stephen Ambrose chronicled the Eisenhower and Nixon presidencies.

7 Anne Rice (b.1941)
America's master scribe of horror novels, Rice wrote the *Vampire Chronicles* series.

8 Ellen Degeneres (b.1958)
The famous comedienne hosts a talk show, and has appeared on stage and in movies.

9 Emeril Lagasse (b.1959)
Now a TV personality, Lagasse is renowned as a chef, restaurateur, and author.

10 Harry Connick, Jr. (b.1967)
This award-winning jazz musician is also a movie star.

Left **NOMA** Center **Louisiana Children's Museum** Right **Exhibit at the African-American Museum**

🔟 Museums and Galleries

1 New Orleans Museum of Art

Established in 1911, the New Orleans Museum of Art, or NOMA, is the oldest repository for art in the city. Permanent collections include rare French and American pieces, including Claude Lorrain's *Ideal View of Tivoli*, and a stunning Native American collection. Works by the masters, including Picasso, Renoir, Monet, Gauguin, and Pollock, are also on display. The museum also includes a Sculpture Garden *(see pp8–11)*.

2 Ogden Museum of Southern Art

Set up in 1994, the Ogden Museum's core collection was donated by art-lover Roger Ogden. The huge collection of contemporary art focuses on artists from the South. These include pieces by father and son Benny and George Andrews, and works by famed painter Clementine Hunter. There is an after-hours program on Thursdays with live music and special exhibits *(see p73)*.

Exhibit at Ogden Museum

3 The National World War II Museum

Founded by historian Stephen Ambrose, this museum opened in 2000, the 56th anniversary of the Normandy invasion. It honors more than a million Americans who took part in World War II. The museum also celebrates New Orleans shipbuilder Andrew Higgins and explores the war's amphibious troop invasions *(see p73)*.

4 Contemporary Arts Center

Housed in a stunning 30,000-sq-ft (2,800-sq-m) building, the Contemporary Arts Center (CAC) honors an eclectic collection of art genres covering music and dance, kinetic sculpture, drawings, and paintings. The CAC also hosts multi-disciplinary workshops in the performing arts *(see p74)*.

5 Confederate Memorial Hall

Veterans of the Civil War have donated most of the memorabilia housed in this museum. Founded in 1891, the Confederate Memorial Hall has a collection of American flags, uniforms, artwork, weaponry, and more than 500 rare photographs including tintypes.
Ⓢ 929 Camp St • Map Q3 • 504-523-4522 • 10am–4pm Tue–Sat • Adm • www. confederatemuseum.com

6 Louisiana State Museum

Five historic French Quarter properties – The Cabildo, The Presbytère *(see pp24–5)*, the 1850 House, the Old U.S. Mint *(see p92)*, and Madame John's

For more information on museums in the city, visit www.neworleansmuseums.com

Legacy – make up the Louisiana State Museum. Collectively, they house thousands of exhibits that trace Louisiana's history from the 18th century onward.

Poster at Louisiana Children's Museum

7 Louisiana Children's Museum

An artfully renovated, multi-level facility, the Louisiana Children's Museum offers a hands-on art and craft experience for children, with interactive exhibits and participatory activities for the whole family. They also offer interesting outreach programs that make classroom teaching more vibrant (see p76).

8 New Orleans African-American Museum

Located in Treme, home to the oldest surviving African-American community in the country, the museum is housed in a lovely Creole villa dating back to 1828. Rotating exhibits chart the art, history, and culture of African-Americans in New Orleans and the diaspora. Highlights include original African beads, masks, musical instruments, and religious objects from the Democratic Republic of Congo. ◈ 1418 Governor Nicholls St. • 504-566-1136 • 11am–4pm Wed–Sat • Adm

9 Italian-American Museum

Italian-Americans have played a major role in the history of New Orleans, and this museum is dedicated to them. The museum has newspapers, artworks, naturalization records of Italians who emigrated to New Orleans. There is also a music library where visitors can listen to classic Dixieland jazz, pioneered by Italian-Americans in the early 20th century. ◈ 537 S. Peters St. • Map P4 • 504-522-7294 • 10am–4pm Tue–Fri • www.american-italianmuseum.com

10 Historic New Orleans Collection

Used mainly as a resource by serious researchers, the Historic New Orleans Collection also attracts curious visitors who can learn about the city through its historical artifacts. Established in 1966, the Historic New Orleans Collection is a repository of manuscripts, artistic exhibits, and documents showcasing the varied cultures that have shaped the city (see p96).

Left **Detail, Supreme Court Building** Center **Lafitte's Blacksmith Shop** Right **The Cabildo**

Architectural Highlights

1 Mercedes-Benz Superdome

This stadium is home to the New Orleans Saints football team. The dome covers the world's largest steel-constructed room unobstructed by posts. Considered to be one of the premier sports venues in the country, the stadium has hosted six National Football League Super Bowls (see p74).

2 Louisiana Supreme Court

The Louisiana Supreme Court Building is an imposing structure of stone and marble. The 1910 structure is an example of Beaux Arts architecture, with its arched windows and Classical pilasters. Once in ruins, this landmark building was restored to its previous glory with a $50-million renovation (see p14).

3 St. Patrick's Church

The subtle Gothic exterior of the church belies its ornate interior. Built in the early 19th century, the original building was overhauled to create a much grander structure with a 185-ft- (56-m-) high bell tower. The altar, windows, and doorways are in Gothic style, while 16 stunning stained-glass windows form a half dome over the altar (see p76).

4 Napoleon House

This early 19th-century landmark was originally the home of the mayor of New Orleans. In 1821, Mayor Nicholas Girod offered his home as a refuge for Napoleon during the latter's imprisonment at St. Helena (see p97).

5 The Cabildo

One of five properties that comprise the Louisiana State Museum, the Cabildo (see p24) was built in 1795. Although the original building was destroyed in the fire of 1788, it was rebuilt. The Cabildo was the historic site where the Louisiana Purchase was signed in 1803 (see p34).

6 Lafitte's Blacksmith Shop

The oldest building in the French Quarter was built in 1772 by alleged slave-traders Pierre and Jean Lafitte. Considered to be the longest continually operating bar room in the country, it is still lit by candlelight (see p28).

Grand bell tower at St. Patrick's Church

New Orleans' Top 10

7 Pontalba Apartment Buildings

In 1849 the French Baroness Pontalba came to New Orleans and built these apartments on inherited land. The oldest apartment buildings in the U.S. are three-story row houses which reflect French and American architecture, with cast-iron galleries and Creole-style floor plans (see p24).

Part of the Pontalba Apartment Buildings

8 Hotel Monteleone

This historic luxury hotel underwent a $60-million renovation in 2004, but retained its original grandeur and charm, while adding modern conveniences (see p14).

9 The Peristyle at City Park

The Neo-Classical Peristyle was built in 1907. It is supported by massive Ionic columns and "guarded" by four cement lions. A stairway leads down to the surrounding Bayou Metairie, a picturesque waterway running through the park. ◆ 1 Palm Drive • Map H2 • 504-482-4888 • www.neworleanscitypark.com

10 Whitney Wyndham Hotel

Originally a bank, this stately structure was converted into a hotel in 2000. It retains the ornate columns, chandeliers, and bank vault from the old building. ◆ 610 Poydras Street • Map P3 • 504-581-4222 • www.wyndham.com

Top 10 Public Art Sites

1 Sydney & Walda Besthoff Sculpture Garden

The Sculpture Garden is an outdoor installation at NOMA (see pp8–11).

2 Enrique Alferez Sculptures

These sculptures are artfully placed throughout the New Orleans City Park (see pp26–7).

3 Train Garden at Botanical Gardens

This exhibit features an eye-level New Orleans cityscape and running miniature train (see p27).

4 "Ocean Song" Kinetic Sculpture

Eight pyramids depicting the movement of the Mississippi. ◆ Woldenberg Park • Map N5

5 Louis Armstrong Statue

The jazz legend is immortalized in this 12-ft- (4-m-) high statue in Armstrong Park (see p89).

6 Robert E. Lee Statue

This sky-high statue honors General Robert E. Lee. ◆ Lee Circle • Map Q2

7 Joan of Arc Maid of Orleans Statue

This golden bronze statue is a replica of a 19th-century sculpture by Emmanuel Frémiet (see p92).

8 Murals at Sazerac Bar

The Art Deco murals in the Roosevelt Hotel bar date to the 1930s (see p119).

9 Auseklis Ozols Murals at Windsor Court Hotel

These murals depict famous New Orleanians in the Grill Room of the hotel (see p119).

10 Blaine Kern's Mardi Gras World

Watch carnival floats and figures being made at this warehouse (see p56).

Left **Shops at Canal Place** Center **Vegetables, French Market** Right **Clock outside Adler's Jewelry**

TOP 10 Shops and Markets

1 Shops at Canal Place

This downtown multi-purpose center located on the edge of the French Quarter offers a choice of theaters, cafés, restaurants, and chic upscale retailers. Shoppers can easily spend a whole day browsing stores such as the multi-level Saks Fifth Avenue, Pottery Barn, Brooks Brothers, Ann Taylor, and Coach, among others *(see p30)*.

2 Riverwalk Marketplace

Locally owned businesses and national retailers blend nicely in this large waterfront complex. This mall built on the site of the 1984 Louisiana World Exposition *(see p35)* offers tax-free shopping for international visitors looking for souvenirs, clothing, home-decor items, and even high-tech games. There are also several restaurants, bars, and fast food joints here *(see p21)*.

3 Rubensteins

Since 1924, Rubenstein Brothers has been one of the most respected purveyors of menswear in New Orleans. Detailed tailoring and personal attention define the service here *(see p31)*.

4 Fleur de Paris

Known internationally for its custom millinery and couture gowns, Fleur de Paris is located in one of the city's most historic

buildings. European-trained milliners create exquisite one-of-a-kind hats on site, with antique flowers, feathers and silk ribbons *(see p15)*.

5 Vive La France

The rich French heritage of New Orleans is evident in home decor items at Vive la France. Here buyers will find glassware, tabletop items, distinctive clocks, a variety of curios, and a richly detailed and rather unusual collection of absinthe-related pieces. 🏵 823 Royal St. • Map L4 • 504-523-0903

6 Adler's Jewelry

Around since 1898, Adler's has been the top jeweler in New Orleans for over a century. Owned by the same family that founded it, buyers from around the world come here to find unique pieces. They have an extensive giftware line as well as a range of locally inspired items, such as New Orleans-themed holiday ornaments and Mardi Gras jewelry *(see p78)*.

Entrance to the Riverwalk Marketplace

7 The French Market

Just at the edge of the Mississippi River, the picturesque French Market is a conglomeration of an outdoor farmer's market, a covered flea market, shops, arts and crafts boutiques, and restaurants. The market is also the site of a number of special events, concerts, and festivals throughout the year *(see p91)*.

8 Belladonna Day Spa and Retail Therapy

On ground level, Belladonna sells everything from books to textiles, perfumes, stationery, tabletop items, and home decor items. Shopping here, in the Zen-like atmosphere, is relaxing enough, but go upstairs and trained professionals are ready to provide massages, facials, and expertly executed spa treatments *(see p70)*.

9 Mignon Faget

Original jewelry items designed by Mignon Faget are on sale in this store, named for her. Her elegant and sometimes quirky designs are inspired by the natural surroundings and man-made structures of New Orleans. The store also stocks beautiful home-decor pieces including glassware, linens, as well as unique baby gifts *(see p70)*.

10 Whole Foods Market

This market is one of many across the country, and deals primarily in organic products with a large selection of seasonal fruits, vegetables, meat, poultry, cheese, bread, wine, and wellness products sourced from local farmers and producers. Shop for groceries or dine at any of the delis or food stalls. ✆ 5600 Magazine St. • Map B6 • 504-899-9119

Top 10 Souvenirs and Keepsakes

1 Mardi Gras Beads

Although they are usually made of plastic, the Mardi Gras beads caught from float-riders are like gold.

2 Ceramic Masks

The tradition of Mardi Gras masking is enshrined in locally made keepsake masks.

3 Voodoo Dolls

These exquisitely detailed figures are sold all over. They are colorful representations of the voodoo tradition.

4 Bourbon Street T-Shirts

There are souvenir t-shirt shops on most blocks in the French Quarter.

5 New Orleans Coffee Beans

The best local coffees are made by Community Coffee and Luzianne and are sold all over the city.

6 Jambalaya Mix

A great way to take home a taste of New Orleans is with the Cajun food producer Zatarain's jambalaya mix.

7 Red Beans and Rice Mix

Delicious and easy to make, red beans and rice is the official dish of New Orleans.

8 Cajun Spices

Chefs like Emeril Lagasse and others take pride in their secret spice mixtures, available for sale citywide.

9 Pat O'Brien's Hurricane Glass

Pat O'Brien's bar mixes powerful "Hurricane" drinks. Guests even get to keep the glass *(see p28)*.

10 Restaurant Cookbooks

The best chefs in town have their own cookbooks, which are usually for sale in their own restaurants.

New Orleans' Top 10

Left **Mahalia Jackson Theater of the Performing Arts** Right **Contemporary Arts Center**

🔟 Performing Arts Venues

1 Rivertown Theatre

Located in the suburb of Kenner, Rivertown Theatre offers dramas, comedies, and Broadway musicals in its 300-seat facility. It has a good mix of community theater and professional productions, featuring everything from Agatha Christie whodunits to Tony-award-winning blockbusters. Ⓢ *325 Minor St.* • *504-468-7221* • *www.rivertown-repertorytheatre.org*

2 Lupin Theater, Tulane University

The Shakespeare Festival at Tulane is the only professional theater event in the South that is dedicated to performing the works of Shakespeare. Performances take place here every summer. The Lupin Theater also schedules arts in education programs through the year. Ⓢ *McWilliams Hall, Tulane University* • *Map B5* • *504-865-5105* • *www.neworleansshakespeare.com*

3 Mahalia Jackson Theater of the Performing Arts

This 2,100-seat theater, named for the famous gospel queen, is located on Basin Street. On any given night in the theater, the audience can experience the Louisiana Philharmonic Orchestra, top-name artists, Broadway companies, ballet troupes, and other performers *(see p89)*.

4 Stage Door Canteen

Located in the National World War II Museum *(see p73)*, the Stage Door Canteen is an entertainment and dining venue. Matinee and evening performances include big bands, musical productions, swing dancing, comedy, and jazz nights. Ⓢ *945 Magazine St.* • *Map Q3* • *504-528-1943* • *www.nationalww2museum.org*

5 Southern Repertory Theater

Situated on the third floor of the Shops at Canal Place *(see p30)*, this theater hosts play readings, dramas, comedies, and musicals. Ⓢ *365 Canal St.* • *Map N4* • *504-522-6545* • *www.southernrep.com*

6 New Orleans Center for Creative Arts (NOCCA)

The city's professional arts school, NOCCA includes a state-of-the-art theater that hosts surprisingly professional productions. Ⓢ *2800 Chartres St.* • *504-940-2787* • *www.nocca.com*

A band performing at the Stage Door Canteen

Contemporary Arts Center (CAC)

Among the many attractions at the CAC is an intimate theater that features musical artists, original stage plays, big-band concerts, and emerging performance artists. The venue is often the setting for cutting-edge performances not common in other local theaters (see p74).

University of New Orleans Lakefront Arena

The Lakefront Arena is a 5,000-seat venue that has hosted everything from big-name rock and hip-hop artists to colorful Disney stage productions. Artists such as Christina Aguilera, Lynyrd Skynyrd, Motley Crue, and Kelly Clarkson have taken the stage here. ✆ 6801 Franklin Ave. • 504-280-7222 • www.arena.uno.edu

New Orleans Arena

An aerial view makes the arena look like a smaller version of the Mercedes-Benz Superdome. The arena is a 17,000-seat facility that often hosts sporting events, but doubles as a venue for major-name entertainers such as Elton John, Billy Joel, and Celine Dion. ✆ 1501 Girod St. • Map P1 • 504-587-3822 • www.neworleansarena.com

The Shadowbox Theatre

An intimate theater space in the Marigny/Bywater area, the Shawdowbox Theatre is the place where fringe and original works are showcased. The theater seats a maximum of 85 people, and its walls are adorned with red velvet curtains. Classes held at the theater help budding actors and musicians develop their talents. ✆ 2400 St. Claude Ave. • 504-298-8676 • www.theshadowboxtheatre.com

Top 10 Movies Filmed in New Orleans

1 A Streetcar Named Desire (1951)
This film, based on Tennessee Williams's play, has stunning performances by Marlon Brando and Vivien Leigh.

2 Easy Rider (1969)
Counterculture bikers travel from Los Angeles to New Orleans searching for freedom in this iconic film.

3 Pretty Baby (1978)
Twelve-year-old Brooke Shields stars in this controversial picture about Storyville, New Orleans' red-light district.

4 Steel Magnolias (1989)
A touching movie about the bond between a group of Southern women.

5 Sex, Lies & Videotape (1989)
Highly erotic, this movie showed the sultry sensuality of New Orleans.

6 JFK (1991)
This Oliver Stone production dealt with the controversies around the killing of John F. Kennedy.

7 The Pelican Brief (1993)
The city figured prominently in this riveting tale of a student who uncovers a conspiracy.

8 Interview With a Vampire (1994)
Anne Rice's tale of the vampire Lestat de Lioncourt starred Tom Cruise, Brad Pitt, and Antonio Banderas.

9 Dead Man Walking (1995)
In this movie, Helen Prejean, a New Orleans nun, fights to abolish the death penalty.

10 Ray (2004)
Academy-award-winning movie on the life of jazz pianist Ray Charles.

Left **Jimmy Buffett's Margaritaville** Center **Maple Leaf Bar** Right **Pat O'Brien's Hurricane**

TOP 10 Live Music Venues

1 Tipitina's
On an otherwise quiet, nondescript uptown corner, Tipitina's rocks the night away with some of the hottest jazz and rock acts in Louisiana. Big-name bands and solo artists from all over the world have performed at this tiny neighborhood pub. ✪ *501 Napoleon Ave. • Map C6 • 504-895-8477*

2 Mid-City Lanes Rock 'n Bowl
This is a bowling alley that doubles as a music and dance venue. Go bowling, and then stay on for a live show and great food, and then dance until the wee hours of the morning. ✪ *3000 South Carrollton Ave. • Map B3 • 504-861-1700*

3 Jimmy Buffett's Margaritaville
Named for its laid-back crooner and founder, Margaritaville has a surprisingly tasty menu as well as some great acts, ranging from mellow guitarists to reggae to progressive rock artists. The pina colada is particularly popular. ✪ *1104 Decatur St. • Map L5 • 504-592-2565*

4 Howlin' Wolf
This club, named for bluesman Chester Burnett, or "Howlin' Wolf," rocks all night and is known for attracting big names such as Harry Connick, Jr., Arturo Sandoval, Allison Krause, Foo Fighters, Dr. John, and many more. The unique carved bar is from a hotel once owned by the famed gangster Al Capone. ✪ *907 St. Peters St. • Map Q4 • 504-522-9653*

5 Maple Leaf Bar
The Maple Leaf Bar attracts an eclectic crowd of college students and people in their 30s and 40s. Big names, such as the Rebirth Brass Band, perform here, but it also promotes upcoming musicians. ✪ *8316 Oak St. • Map A4 • 504-866-9359*

6 Pat O'Brien's
Guests will probably have to wait to get in, but the queue is as much fun as it is inside. The music is lively and the Hurricane is the most popular cocktail. The courtyard restaurant should not be missed either *(see p28)*.

7 Davenport Lounge
Upscale, laid-back luxury characterizes this lobby-level lounge at the Ritz-Carlton, one of

Guests enjoying a dance at Tipitina's

the city's finest hotels *(see p30)*. Furnished with 19th-century antiques, the lounge offers an elegant afternoon tea during the day and live music every evening. The Davenport Lounge is named for famous jazz trumpetist and singer Jeremy Davenport who provides the evening's entertainment.

Cat's Meow Karaoke Club

Around since 1989, this high-energy club is located on one of the busiest corners of Bourbon Street. Cat's Meow is open on all sides so passers-by can witness non-stop karaoke as it happens. Guests can also enjoy cocktails in the courtyard of the club *(see p29)*.

Patrons outside Cat's Meow

Krazy Korner

Rhythm and blues have been the calling card of this place since the 1950s. The club stays open all night and cover bands often play classic rock, ideal for dancing. The club's balcony is an added plus. ◎ *640 Bourbon St.* • *Map L4* • *504-524-3157*

Mulate's Cajun Restaurant and Dance Hall

Located in the heart of the Warehouse District, this place is as much a restaurant as it is a dance hall, serving real Cajun-style food accompanied by authentic Cajun music. Highlights are the seafood gumbo and the Cajun seafood platter *(see p76)*.

Top 10 Jazz Clubs

1 Snug Harbor
Truly a jazz musician's club, Snug Harbor also serves decent food. ◎ *626 Frenchmen St.* • *Map K6* • *504-949-0696*

2 Arnaud's
This intimate dining room has live Dixieland jazz along with a selected "jazz" menu at a fixed price *(see p101)*.

3 Palm Court Jazz Café
Live traditional jazz and well-executed Creole cuisine characterize this café. ◎ *1204 Decatur St.* • *Map L5* • *504-525-0200*

4 Sweet Lorraine's
Stellar sound system, great atmosphere, and the best jazz in town, all under one roof. ◎ *1931 St. Claude Ave.* • *Map K4* • *504-945-9654*

5 The Three Muses
This place is known for local jazz and its great cocktail menu. ◎ *536 Frenchmen St.* • *Map K6* • *504-298-8746*

6 Preservation Hall
This music hall is a venue dedicated to preserving the classic New Orleans jazz tradition *(see p29)*.

7 Fritzel's European Jazz Pub
Since 1969, this jazz hub has attracted the best musicians. ◎ *733 Bourbon St.* • *Map L4* • *504-586-4800*

8 The Bombay Club
Clubby and classy, this club has live music every weekend. ◎ *830 Conti St.* • *Map M3* • *504-586-0972*

9 House of Blues
World-renowned musicians play here. ◎ *225 Decatur St.* • *Map N4* • *504-310-4999*

10 Maison Bourbon
Renowned for its diesel-strength mojitos and traditional Southern jazz. ◎ *641 Bourbon St.* • *Map L4* • *504-522-8818*

Left **Napoleon's Itch sign** Right **Good Friends Bar**

Gay and Lesbian Venues

1 OZ
One of the city's most popular dance clubs, OZ is a gay venue with a vibrant atmosphere. It has a fantastic sound system, great DJs, and several fun weekly events. These include Drag Bingo, or "Dingo," Boy Next Door contests, theme performances, and daily happy hours from 4 to 8pm. Thursday is the liveliest night of the week – billed as the "Totally Awesome 80s night", it is complete with a male strip show at midnight *(see p100)*.

2 Big Daddy's
A bit off the beaten path, Big Daddy's is a small neighborhood lounge bar with an intimate atmosphere. Located in the Faubourg Marigny, the place is bustling on Sunday afternoons with live entertainment. Big Daddy's also has some of the friendliest and most well-liked bartenders in the city. ⊗ 2513 Royal St. • 504-948-6288

3 The Country Club
Housed in an elegant Creole-style mansion in the Faubourg Marigny, The Country Club offers relaxation as well as an exciting nightlife. Visitors can choose from a number of options, including a restaurant offering traditional New Orleans cuisine, a bar, pool, Jacuzzi, a large movie screen, spa, massage services, and a veranda, which is perfect for enjoying cocktails. Nude sunbathing as well as pool and hot-tub parties are among the club's attractions. ⊗ 634 Louisa St. • 504-945-0742

4 Napoleon's Itch
Located in Bourbon Street, the center of gay nightlife, Napoleon's Itch is a quiet, upscale bar. The only smoke-free club in the city, it has a sleek, contemporary interior and is a perfect place to relax with a martini or a beer from the extensive menu. ⊗ 734 Bourbon St. • Map L4 • 504-371-5450

5 Bourbon Pub-Parade Disco
This pub is regarded as the anchor of the gay and lesbian entertainment district in New Orleans. The Bourbon Pub-Parade Disco is the biggest, as well as the longest continuously operating, gay club in the country. The pub downstairs is packed with patrons watching videos on large screens. Upstairs, the raucous Parade disco has a

Exterior of Bourbon Pub-Parade Disco

dance floor and a variety of live entertainment, including contests, cabarets, and male dancers. ◈ 801 Bourbon St. • Map L4 • 504-529-2107

Good Friends Bar
A slightly older crowd frequents Good Friends Bar. Tuesday nights mean karaoke, and on Sunday evenings, the Queen's Head Pub upstairs has a piano bar sing-along. ◈ 740 Dauphine St. • Map L4 • 504-566-7191

Rawhide
This gay leather bar, despite being slightly rough-edged, is known for its exciting parties. Rawhide is dimly lit, and has pool tables and poker machines. The general ambience of the place makes it an active meet and play area. ◈ 740 Burgundy St. • Map L4 • 504-525-8106

The Phoenix
The Phoenix is one of the most frequented leather bars for the gay community of New Orleans. The Eagle Bar, upstairs, is a popular meeting spot for locals. This place is packed every Friday and Saturday night. ◈ 941 Elysian Fields Ave. • Map K6 • 504-945-9264

Interior of Café Lafitte in Exile

Café Lafitte in Exile
Lafitte's is the oldest gay club in the country and was the one-time haunt of Tennessee Williams. Today, the club has two floors of state-of-the-art sound systems and screens for playing videos. Lafitte's balcony is one of the most coveted spots, especially during Mardi Gras. The Wednesday night karaoke and weekly "Trash Disco" is a huge draw. ◈ 901 Bourbon St. • Map L4 • 504-522-8397

The Friendly Bar
This bar is true to its name with a congenial atmosphere and friendly bartenders who always greet guests. The DJ plays good music and the lively pool table and friendly banter makes this a great place in which to relax over a beer. ◈ 2301 Chartres St. • Map K6 • 504-943-8929

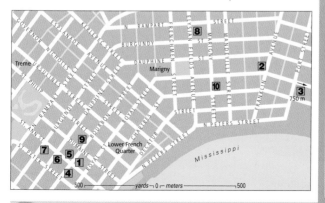

Left **Alligator sauce piquante** Center **Restaurant serving Po' boys** Right **Barbecued shrimp**

🔟 Regional Dishes

1 Alligator Sauce Piquante
Traditionally, Cajuns used spicy sauce piquante in dishes made with rabbit. Alligator sauce piquante is a variation that uses the tail meat of an alligator, combined with heavy seasonings, including cayenne pepper, garlic, green chilies, onions, black pepper, and jalapeno peppers.

A typical *muffuletta*

2 Court Bouillion
A staple in Louisiana Cajun households, court bouillion is essentially a seafood stew, but there are several variations. The two most popular use redfish or catfish. The recipe always features garlic, onion, and celery. Learning to cook this dish takes time and requires a lot of practice.

3 Blackened Redfish
Local chef Paul Prudhomme popularized the blackening cooking style. The redfish recipe calls for the fish to be rubbed with Cajun spices and then cooked on high heat in a cast-iron skillet. The process is often used for chicken, catfish, and other meats and fish.

4 Oysters Bienville
Named after the founder of New Orleans, this unique dish was created during the Great Depression at Antoine's, the oldest family-run restaurant in the country. The oysters are topped with béchamel, sherry, cayenne, garlic, shallots, and minced shrimp and then baked on rock salt with a bread-crumb and cheese topping.

5 Barbecued Shrimp
Not to be confused with foods cooked in bottled barbecue sauces, these shrimps are smoked and then cooked with Worcestershire sauce and black pepper. The best dishes are with jumbo Gulf shrimps, which are then slow cooked. The secret to making delicious shrimp is by using a generous amount of real butter.

6 Fried Green Tomatoes with Shrimp Rémoulade
Green tomatoes have a rich flavor, but in New Orleans, the taste is enhanced by frying them in batter and adding fresh Gulf shrimps and tangy rémoulade sauce. It is a staple dish in the best restaurants of New Orleans.

Oysters on ice in a restaurant

Preceding pages **Aerial view, Louisiana Superdome**

7 Seafood Gumbo

Gumbo can be safely called the official food of New Orleans (next to red beans and rice, of course). Gumbo is a rich, thick dark soup with mixtures of seafood, such as crab, shrimp, catfish, oysters, or whatever the cook desires. It can also be made with chicken or sausage.

8 Jambalaya

Both French and Spanish influences have shaped the jambalaya. This rice-based Creole dish is a bit like paella. Some make it with seafood, while others make it with chicken, sausages, or both. Tomatoes, celery, and even-handed seasoning are all key to perfecting this dish.

A colorful jambalaya

9 Muffuletta

Legend has it that New Orleans' old Central Grocery was a gathering spot for local workers. Holding bread in one hand and meat in another, they would engage in lively debates, and food would fly. The owner eventually put the ingredients between bread, added olive salad and invented the *muffuletta*.

10 Po' Boys

Sandwiches made of crispy French bread with ingredients such as shrimp, catfish, oysters, beef, ham, crab, and even French fries. Ubiquitous in New Orleans.

Top 10 Drinks

1 Sazerac

Dating to the Civil War, this cocktail contains Cognac, rye, herbsaint (or absinthe), and bitters.

2 Mint Julep

Iconic in the American South, mint juleps are a refreshing mix of bourbon, mint, sugar, and water.

3 Ramos Gin Fizz

Also called New Orleans Fizz, Ramos Gin Fizz includes gin, lemon, lime, egg white, cream, sugar, orange-flower water, and soda.

4 Hurricane

This powerful sweet rum drink is the signature cocktail at the French Quarter's Pat O'Brien's bar *(see p28)*.

5 Cajun Martini

Simply adding a shot of jalapeno-infused vodka turns an ordinary Martini into a hot and spicy sensation.

6 Mimosa

The Sunday brunch drink of choice is a mixture of fresh orange juice and champagne.

7 Abita Beer

Brewed in nearby Abita Springs, Louisiana, Abita has eight flagship brews and five seasonal brews.

8 Pimm's Cup

This summery New Orleans favorite gin-based cocktail was invented in 19th-century England as a health tonic.

9 Dixie Beer

Dixie has brewed beer in New Orleans for 100 years, and it is sold all over town.

10 Cajun Bloody Mary

Not just any old Bloody Mary will do – people in New Orleans add hot sauce and horseradish to this classic cocktail.

Left **Commander's Palace** Center **August** Right **Gumbo dish at Mr B's Bistro**

🔟 Restaurants

1 Commander's Palace
Known for its impeccable service and gracious ambience, Commander's excels with the house turtle soup, crab cakes, and its signature white chocolate bread pudding. Ask for a table in the Garden Room *(see p71)*.

2 Brigtsen's
Frank Brigtsen worked in some of the city's finest kitchens before opening his own Creole restaurant in a quaint uptown house. Brigtsen's excels with full-flavored comfort food dishes such as roast duck and sesame crusted pork tenderloin.
🔸 *723 Dante St. • Map A4 • 504-861-7610 • $$$$*

3 Stella!
Chef/owner Scott Boswell calls his distinctive cooking "Global/Modern cuisine." In his intimate, upscale dining room he serves his guests unique preparations such as Canadian lobster risotto or duck prepared in five different ways. The experience is pricey, but worth it *(see p93)*.

Exterior of Stella!

4 Arnaud's
This restaurant has served the city for more than 80 years. The classically Creole menu is matched by the elegant, ambience. Shrimp Arnaud appetizer, oysters Bienville, and speckled trout Amandine are specialties here. Go upstairs to see the Mardi Gras museum *(see p101)*.

5 Mosca's
A little roadhouse off the beaten path, Mosca's serves the best Italian food in town. Standouts are oysters Mosca, chicken à La Grande and spaghetti Bordelaise. The restaurant accepts cash only. 🔸 *4137 Hwy. 90 West • 504-436-9942 • $$$*

6 August
This is the flagship restaurant of one of the city's renowned chefs, John Besh. Upscale, elegant and centrally located, this downtown eatery features creative dishes such as pan-roasted sable fish with truffled potatoes. Besh is known for his use of special seasonings and local ingredients. 🔸 *301 Tchoupitoulas St. • Map P4 • 504-299-9777 • $$$$$*

7 The Grill Room
The Grill Room is among the top fine-dining spots in New Orleans. Housed in the swanky Windsor Court Hotel *(see p119)*, the menu has four parts: Indulge, Southern,

Recommend your favorite restaurant on **traveldk.com**

Steakhouse, and Unadulterated. Grilled foie gras and lobster, and the truffled risotto are the highlights. It also boasts a superb wine list. ◎ *Windsor Court Hotel, 300 Gravier Street • Map P4 • 504-522-1994 • $$$$$ • www.windsorcourthotel.com*

Eleven 79
A small, classy Italian eatery with soft lighting and music, Eleven 79 also boasts great wines, seasoned waiters, and a menu that beguiles the clientele to return. The experience at this restaurant is completely authentic. ◎ *1179 Annunciation St. • Map R3 • 504-299-1179 • $$$$*

The classy interior at Galatoire's Restaurant

Galatoire's Restaurant
A family-owned eatery, Galatoire's has not changed much in terms of its appearance or reputation. Even the menu remains unchanged. The sautéed sweetbread appetizer, crabmeat Sardou and soufflé potatoes are culinary institutions *(see p28)*.

Mr. B's Bistro
Anchoring the corner of Royal and Bienville streets in the French Quarter, this casually elegant bistro made a name for itself with scrumptious dishes such as gumbo ya-ya (made with chicken and spicy sausage) and a honey-ginger glazed pork chop. Sunday brunch is a treat – try the catfish meunière *(see p15)*.

Top 10 Places for Late Night Dining

1 Trolley Stop Café
The ideal place for gooey egg dishes, waffles, and burgers. ◎ *1923 St. Charles Ave. • Map S1 • 504-523-0090 • $$*

2 Port of Call
Burgers are huge and the large Monsoon cocktail is a killer. ◎ *838 Esplanade Ave. • Map K5 • 504-523-0120 • $$*

3 Fiorella's
At Fiorella's, it is all about fried chicken and red beans and rice *(see p93)*.

4 Camellia Grill
Sit at the counter for fried apple pie, cheeseburgers, chili and crispy French fries. ◎ *626 S. Carrollton Ave. • Map A4 • 504-309-2679 • $*

5 Clover Grill
Burgers, fries, and other late night indulgences are on offer. ◎ *900 Bourbon St. • Map L4 • 504-598-1010 • $*

6 Angeli
Salads, pizzas, and pasta make for perfect late night fare. ◎ *1141 Decatur St. • Map L5 • 504-566-0077 • $$*

7 Ernst Café
Come here for typical bar food and great po' boys. ◎ *600 St. Peters St. • Map P4 • 504-525-8544 • $$*

8 Turtle Bay
Pizza, sweet tiramisu, and icy Abita beer are served here. ◎ *1119 Decatur St. • Map L5 • 504-586-0563 • $$*

9 St. Charles Tavern
Roast beef po' boys, sausage biscuits, and pizza are on the menu. ◎ *1433 St. Charles Ave. • Map R2 • 504-523-9823 • $$*

10 La Peniche
Famous for its pancakes, eggs Benedict, and desserts. ◎ *1940 Dauphine St. • Map K5 • 504-943-1460 • $*

 For more restaurants and a key to price categories See p71.

Left **Café Degas** Center **Courtyard in Feelings Café** Right **Bon Ton Café sign**

🔟 Cafés

1 Feelings Café
This intimate restaurant is tucked away in a residential area. The lively piano bar and elegant outdoor courtyard would be reason enough to visit, but the real enticement is the chef's seafood stuffed eggplant with shrimp, crawfish, and sausage. 🅂 *2600 Chartres St. • Map F3 • 504-945-2222*

2 Café du Monde
Since 1862, New Orleanians have relied on Café du Monde for their morning coffee with chicory and *beignets* (fried pastries with powdered sugar), a New Orleans specialty. Starting off as a small stall in the French Market *(see p91)*, today the café has multiple locations, but the anchor restaurant is still in the French Quarter. 🅂 *800 Decatur St. • Map L5 • 504-525-4544*

3 Café Degas
For a true French café experience, head to Café Degas. Named after French Impressionist painter Edgar Degas, the restaurant offers everything from a light *hors d'oeuvres* menu and a stellar Salad Nicoise, to a perfect Dijon-crusted rack of lamb *(see p85)*.

4 Blue Plate Café
Nestled in a residential neighborhood, the Blue Plate Café is packed everyday for breakfast and lunch. Burgers, creative sandwiches and salads, home-made soups, and windows overlooking the charming neighborhood make this a popular stop for many regular customers. The daily specials are quite good. 🅂 *1330 Prytania St. • Map R2 • 504-309-9500*

5 La Madeleine Bakery Café
It is hard to know which is more irresistible at La Madeleine – the elegantly presented pastry selection – or the hearty home-made soups. La Madeleine, ostensibly a bakery, turns out some outstanding hot entrées, pastas, and chicken dishes. It also offers one of the best cups of coffee in town. 🅂 *601 S. Carrollton Ave. • Map A4 • 504-861-8662*

6 Café Roma
In a town where pizza has slowly emerged as a culinary art form, Café Roma has been offering some of the best pizzas for decades. The menu also includes salads and sandwiches, but the pesto-artichoke pizza is the bestseller. 🅂 *1901 Sophie Wright Place • Map J5 • 504-524-2419*

Colorful exterior of Blue Plate Café

Vic's Kangaroo Café
Known for its 11 beers on tap and its lively atmosphere, Vic's is usually loud and crowded. They have some great Australian specialties on the menu as well. 🕲 636 Tchoupitoulas St. • Map P4 • 504-524-4329

Café Rani
Noted for its salads, Café Rani has a lovely outdoor courtyard and an artfully designed interior. Salads are generously portioned and paired nicely with a limited selection of well-chosen wines. 🕲 2917 Magazine St. • Map H6 • 504-895-2500

Chic interiors of Café Rani

Bon Ton Café
The Bon Ton has been in the business since the early 1900s. Local specialties such as turtle soup, gumbo, and crabmeat *au gratin* share menu space with a respectable selection of steaks and chops. The bread pudding with whiskey sauce is a must. 🕲 401 Magazine St. • Map P3 • 504-524-3386

Café Amelie
Sunday brunch at Café Amelie is served in its strikingly beautiful courtyard. The menu is limited but expertly executed, and the ambience is second to none. The highlights include the pan-fried crab cakes with a citrus drizzle. 🕲 912 Royal St. • Map L5 • 504-412-8965

Top 10 Breakfast Spots

Dante's Kitchen
The Mississippi blueberry pancakes served here are a must-try. Open for breakfasts on Sundays (see p71).

La Peniche
The restaurant offers great egg dishes. Try their special eggs Benedict (see p53).

Lil' Dizzy's Café
The menu consists of Creole soul food. Regional fare is served for breakfast as well. 🕲 610 Poydras St. • Map P3 • 504-212-5656

Café Adelaide
For a typically Southern breakfast try Café Adelaide's honeycomb waffles with toasted pecan syrup (see p79).

Brennan's Restaurant
The only place to suggest a wine with every breakfast entrée (see p14).

Eat
From the grillades to the fresh bagels, the breakfast is hearty here. 🕲 900 Dumaine St. • Map L4 • 504-522-7222

Slim Goodies Diner
This place offers hearty eggs, meat, and potatoes breakfasts. 🕲 3322 Magazine St. • Map G6 • 504-891-3447

Camellia Grill
The omelettes here are grilled right in front of guests. The chef's special omelette with ham, bacon, and cheese is a must try (see p53).

Trolley Stop
This place looks like a streetcar and the food is delicious. 🕲 1923 St. Charles Ave. • Map S1 • 504-523-0090

Mother's
Eggs any style and the resturant's special fresh biscuits with meat start the day. 🕲 401 Poydras St. • Map P4 • 504-523-9656

New Orleans' Top 10

Left **Louisiana Children's Museum** Center **Audubon Zoo** Right **Exhibit at Mardi Gras World**

TOP 10 Children's Attractions

1 Audubon Zoo

To make the most of an excursion to the Audubon Zoo, spend the whole day there. Take a ride on the Endangered Species Carousel, the Swamp Train, or the Safari Simulator Ride, which moves in sync with images that are projected on to a screen. Viewing the animals in their simulated natural habitats is an entertaining and educational experience. The Audubon Zoo houses rare white tigers, orangutans, elephants, giraffes, bears, and alligators among others *(see pp12–13)*.

2 Aquarium of the Americas

Located at the edge of the Mississippi River, the aquarium houses approximately 15,000 aquatic creatures and nearly 600 species. Do not miss the 30-ft- (9-m-) long Caribbean Reef Tunnel, which allows a view of underwater life usually reserved for divers. Also visit the Seahorse Gallery *(see pp18–19)*.

Gulf of Mexico exhibit at the Aquarium of the Americas

3 Louisiana Children's Museum

Although an educational venue for children, this museum also appeals to inquisitive and playful adults. Wonderful interactive displays, such as the Little Port of New Orleans, or the Eye to Eye (where you can step inside a giant eyeball), makes this a novel way to learn *(see p76)*.

4 Blaine Kern's Mardi Gras World

This enormous warehouse displays all kinds of Mardi Gras trivia and memorabilia. Most of the exhibits, including costumes and floats, are part of artist Blaine Kern's collection and are created by him. Watching the artists and builders at work can be quite a magical experience.
🅂 *1380 Port of New Orleans Place • Map S5 • 504-361-7821 • 9:30am–4:30pm daily • Adm • www.mardigrasworld.com*

5 Audubon Insectarium

More than 70 live insect exhibits are on display in this insectarium. As well as real insects, there are also giant animatronic bugs and a special gift shop with insect-themed products. Visitors can also sample insect cuisine at the Bug Appetit café or watch butterflies in the Asian garden *(see p31)*.

6 Jean Lafitte Swamp Tour

New Orleans is surrounded by swamps which are home to varied plants and wildlife. The best way to see this unique ecosystem is from a swamp boat. The tour begins outside New Orleans and is an exciting excursion for families. ◎ *1 Poydras St., Riverwalk Marketplace • Map P4 • 504-689-4186 • Call for rates • www.jeanlafitteswamptour.com*

Giant shoe house at Storyland

7 Storyland

Children can enjoy a bit of old-fashioned fun at City Park's theme playground, Storyland, with its characters and exhibits from fairy tales. These delightful creations include Captain Hook's pirate ship, Pinocchio's whale, and Jack & Jill's hill. The best part is that children can clamber all over the structures and let their imagination run wild. There is also a storybook cottage which is a popular location for children's birthday parties *(see p26)*.

8 Entergy IMAX Theatre

3-D films are shown on a giant five-and-a-half-story screen with a spectacular sound system providing a larger-than-life viewing experience at the Entergy IMAX Theatre. Watch amazing features on underwater adventures, historical re-enactments, real footage of natural disasters, and docu-dramas on nature *(see p21)*.

9 Zephyr Field

Locals call this modern baseball field, located on Airline Drive, the Shrine on Airline. The stadium has 10,000 seats and seating for another 1,000 people on the nearby levee overlooking center field. The $21-million facility built after Hurricane Katrina has added amenities such as a swimming pool, luxury suites, and hot tubs. The stadium is not only for fans of the Zephyr baseball team, but also for culture buffs, as it hosts various kinds of entertainment.
◎ *6000 Airline Dr. • 504-734-5155 • Timings vary by event • Adm • web.minorleaguebaseball.com*

10 Creole Queen

Nothing can give you the true feeling of being in New Orleans as much as a journey down the Mississippi River on a historical paddlewheel steamboat. The cruise is long enough to enjoy the captain's narration, rich with history and anecdotes, as well as see the city from the water. Visitors can also enjoy a dinner buffet and jazz music on the special Creole Queen dinner cruise *(see p20)*.

Storyland's characters were built by Mardi Gras float builders.

Left **Tombs at the Metairie Cemetery** Right **Signboard of OZ**

🔟 Offbeat Activities

1 Red Dress Run
Every year hundreds of men and women outfit themselves in red dresses and run as a huge group through the streets of New Orleans. Known as the Hash House Harriers, the group usually follows a particular trail stopping at most bars along the way. ◈ www.nolareddress.tumblr.com

2 New Orleans Bingo! Show
One of the most entertaining shows in town, the New Orleans Bingo! Show is an interactive multimedia stage experience. This musical gameshow cabaret cleverly combines slapstick comedy, burlesque dancers, bingo games, aerialists, and clowns to thrill audiences with an amazing theatrical performance. ◈ www.neworleansbingoshow.com

3 New Orleans Original Cocktail Tour
This walking tour makes perfect sense in a city known for its cocktails. From the Sazerac to the Hurricane, connoisseurs will enjoy a different view of New Orleans through its history of fine dining and drinking. ◈ Steamboat Natchez Dock • Map M5 • 504-569-1401 • 4pm daily • Adm • www.graylineneworleans.com

4 New Orleans Ghost Tour
Visitors who are really keen to know the dark, hidden secrets of the old French Quarter should not miss the ghost tour. This walking tour explores documented hauntings, ghost sightings, and otherworldly events. The tour guides are often eccentric and theatrical. ◈ 723 St. Peter Street • Map M5 • 504-861-2727 • 6pm and 8pm daily • Adm • www.hauntedhistorytours.com

5 Drag Bingo at OZ
OZ is the hot local gay dance club, and every Sunday it hosts the Drag Bingo when the players and the callers dress in drag and rock the house (see p100).

6 Tour a Cemetery
In New Orleans people are usually buried above ground rather than below. The city is technically below sea level and does not allow digging too deep in some areas. These stunning cemeteries can be found citywide; Metairie Cemetery is particularly well-kept. ◈ Metairie Cemetery, 5100 Pontchartrain Blvd. • 8am–5pm daily

Enthusiasts out on a ghost tour

A Day in the Swamp

7 In New Orleans, a popular tourist attraction is an up-close view of the swamps. These tours leave regularly from outside the city limits taking visitors through the varied topography of a typical Southern swamp. Swamp tours are organized by tour companies such as Jean Lafitte *(see p57)*.

Italian Dinner with Singing Waiters

8 The waiters at Café Giovanni sing opera songs on Wednesday, Friday, and Saturday nights. They are trained opera vocalists, and if anything goes perfectly with meatballs and spaghetti, it is a side of Tosca. ⬧ *117 Decatur St.* • *Map N4* • *504-529-2154*

A Mardi Gras float under construction

Ride in a Mardi Gras Parade

9 Thousands of people ride in one or more of dozens of annual Mardi Gras parades. To ride in a parade, visitors must get a membership of one of the Mardi Gras organizations, or "krewes." Beyond the parade, members are also allowed to participate in all of the krewe's activities.

Visit a Bourbon Street Strip Club

10 The naughty nightlife on Bourbon frequently includes a sneak peek at a strip club. The entire length of Bourbon Street from Canal Street to St. Ann Street has several clubs catering to gentlemen.

Top 10 Spiritual and Voodoo Sites

1 Marie Laveau's House of Voodoo
Have a reading at the house of the voodoo high priestess. ⬧ *739 Bourbon St.* • *Map L4* • *504-581-3751*

2 Voodoo Museum
Explore the mysteries of voodoo in this unique museum. ⬧ *724 Dumaine St.* • *Map L4* • *504-680-0128*

3 Lafayette Cemetery #1
Ann Rice's *Interview With a Vampire* was filmed in this cemetery *(see p68)*.

4 St. Louis Cemetery #1
This is the oldest cemetery in New Orleans. ⬧ *499 Basin St.* • *Map L3*

5 St. Louis Cemetery #2
This extension of St. Louis Cemetery #1 was added in the 19th century. ⬧ *300 N. Claiborne Ave.* • *Map L2* • *504-482-5065*

6 St. Louis Cemetery #3
This elaborate burial ground was built over an old leper colony. ⬧ *3421 Esplanade Ave.* • *Map J2* • *504-482-5065*

7 Voodoo Spiritual Temple
West African spiritual healing is practiced here. ⬧ *828 N. Rampart St.* • *Map L4* • *504-522-9627*

8 Voodoo Authentica Cultural Center & Collection
Experience in-house voodoo rituals here. ⬧ *612 Dumaine St.* • *Map L5* • *504-522-2111*

9 New Orleans Zen Temple
Learn the Buddhist meditative practice of Zazen. ⬧ *748 Camp St.* • *Map P3* • *504-525-3533*

10 New Orleans Voodoo Tour
Visit voodoo altars and learn about the different practitioners. ⬧ *723 St. Peter St.* • *Map M4* • *504-861-2727*

Left **Crowds at the Jazz and Heritage Festival** Right **Revelers at Creole Tomato Festival**

🔟 Festivals and Events

1 Mardi Gras
New Orleans is internationally known for its Carnival celebrations that gear up about three weeks before Lent. Mardi Gras draws a million tourists every year for parades, street parties, and masked balls. The more risqué side of Carnival happens in the French Quarter, while family celebrations happen in neighborhoods all over town *(see pp22–3)*.

A colorful Mardi Gras float

2 French Quarter Festival
Every April for one weekend the French Quarter turns into a 15-square block street party. Stages are set up all over the Quarter for top jazz, rock, hip-hop, and Cajun bands. Local restaurants are represented in booths in Jackson Square and nearby Woldenberg Park serving their signature items. 📞 504-522-5730 • www.frenchquarterfestivals.com

3 Jazz and Heritage Festival
Covering two weekends in April and May, the Jazz Fest as locals refer to it, offers top

performers from all over the world in jazz, gospel, Cajun, zydeco, blues, R&B, rock, funk, African, and Latin music. Look for regional artists and craftsmen displaying their wares and foods. 📞 504-410-4100 • www.nojazzfest.com

4 New Orleans Wine & Food Experience
During the NOWFE, held every May, local restaurants host vintner dinners, while daytime hours are spent in seminars, and cooking demos. The Grand Tasting is a huge event at the Mercedes-Benz Superdome *(see p74)*. 📞 504-529-9463 • www.nowfe.com

5 Creole Tomato Festival
Tomatoes have long been an essential crop in Louisiana. Every June, the French Market *(see p91)* celebrates a festival dedicated to this fruit with cooking demos, art exhibits, music and dancing, and the crowning of the Tomato Queen.

6 Go Fourth on the River
Dueling barges on the Mississippi River offer a spectacular fireworks display on Independence Day (July 4). The fireworks are choreographed in time with stirring patriotic music. 📞 www.go4thontheriver.com

7 Essence Festival
African-American culture is celebrated on the Independence Day weekend every year with the Essence Festival. The

program showcases big name performers, African-American artists, writers, craftsmen, culinary artists, and others. ✪ www.essencemusicfestival.com

Satchmo Summerfest
In early August each year one of the city's favorite sons, Louis "Satchmo" Armstrong, is honored with a festival in his name. Armstrong, one of the preeminent jazz musicians of the 20th century, is heralded with live jazz, educational seminars, and all day partying. ✪ 504-522-5730
• www.fqfi.org

Southern Decadence
One of the largest gay and lesbian events in the country takes place in the French Quarter every September. The weekend event includes a massive costume parade, drag shows, parties, and more. ✪ www.southerndecadence.net

Christmas
Christmas is celebrated citywide with a packed schedule of organized events. Look for gospel performances, concerts at St. Louis Cathedral, Christmas caroling in Jackson Square, and special menus at French Quarter restaurants. ✪ 504-522-5730
• www.frenchquarterfestivals.com

St. Louis Cathedral during Christmas

Top 10 Other Festivals and Events

1 Tennessee Williams Literary Festival
Held in late March, the festival includes panel discussions, theater, music, and fine foods.

2 Ponchatoula Strawberry Festival
A short drive from New Orleans, Ponchatoula hosts a festival featuring music, games, strawberry-eating, and cooking contests every April.

3 Greek Festival
This May event features live Greek music, authentic cuisine, dancers, an outdoor marketplace, and family-friendly activities.

4 Shakespeare Festival
The bard is honored annually (May–Jul) at Tulane University with performances of his works (see p42).

5 Tales of the Cocktail
The history and culture of the cocktail is the centerpiece of this annual July event.

6 White Linen Night
White linen attire is worn during this August street party in the Warehouse District.

7 Bikefest, Motorcycle Rally, & Music Festival
Motorcycle lovers gather in October for the state's biggest rally.

8 Halloween New Orleans™
Every Halloween, the gay community sponsors a party weekend to benefit Lazarus House, an AIDS hospice.

9 Voodoo Music Festival
A Halloween weekend of rock, jazz, and hip hop at New Orleans City Park (see pp26–7).

10 Louisiana Swamp Fest
Enjoy live music and Cajun food at the Audubon Zoo on the first weekend of November (see p12).

Above **Taking a boat ride through the Atchafalaya Basin, St. Martin's Parish**

Excursions and Day Trips

St. Francisville

Time stands still in this small and elegant town, with its historic mansions and gorgeous 19th-century gardens. Lovely bed and breakfasts, restaurants, art galleries, and specialty shops are the attractions of this typical Southern town. Map A1
• www.stfrancisville.us

Houmas House Plantation and Gardens

This beautiful property, dating back to the mid-18th century, was meticulously restored in 2003 by current owner, Kevin Kelly. The Greek Revival mansion is surrounded by lush landscaped grounds. The gift shop stocks classic New Orleans memorabilia and rare books and is a highlight, as is the Latil's Landing Restaurant, which serves old Louisiana cuisine. 40136 Hwy. 942, Darrow • Map B1 • 225-473-9380 • 9am–5pm Mon–Tue, 9am–8pm Wed–Sun • Adm • www.houmashouse.com

St. Martin's Parish

A trip to Louisiana would not be complete without a day spent in Cajun Country. Located in the Atchafalaya Basin, St. Martin's Parish and its surrounding towns form part of a national heritage area. A little over 2 hours' drive west of New Orleans, this region is rich in history and its authentic Cajun and Creole cuisine. Visit during the festive season to enjoy the colorful celebrations. • www.cajuncountry.org

River Road

Often called the Great River Road, this stretch between New Orleans and Baton Rouge is home to many grand plantation houses, most built by wealthy sugar planters. These mansions have been carefully preserved and many of them are available for touring. Map B2

Baton Rouge

The capital city of Louisiana is definitely worth the hour-long drive from New Orleans. Baton Rouge is a thriving metropolis that offers great dining and a bustling nightlife. Visitors can also enjoy boat tours of the river, swamp tours, riverboat casinos, museums, and beautiful vineyards. Map B1 • www. visitbatonrouge.com

Driveway leading up to Houmas House

Oak Alley Plantation

The setting for many major movies and television shows, Oak Alley is a striking plantation property. A canopy of giant oak trees forms an impressive avenue that leads to a Greek-Revival style mansion. ◈ *3645 Highway 18, Vacherie • Map B2 • 225-265-2151 • 9am–4:30pm Mon–Fri, 9am–5pm Sat–Sun • Adm • www.oakalleyplantation.com*

Rosedown

Covering a large area in St. Francisville, the Rosedown Plantation is distinguished by its sprawling formal gardens, which protect a variety of rare plants. This area is preserved as a historic site by the state. ◈ *12501 Hwy. 10, St. Francisville • 225-635-3332 • 9am–5pm daily • Adm • www.crt.state.la.us*

St. Martinville

With only 7,000 residents, St. Martinville, near Lafayette, still retains its small-town flavor and Southern charm. The town hosts the La Grande Boucherie des Cajuns every year in February, which celebrates Cajun culture with feasting and games. The town is also home to an African-American museum which traces the history of slavery in the region. ◈ *Map A1 • www.stmartinville.org*

Musicians performing at a bar in Lafayette

Lafayette

Although a 4-hour drive from New Orleans, Lafayette is a popular weekend getaway. Located in the heart of Cajun Country, this city has a very distinct culture and offers visitors many attractions, including eclectic local cuisine, a national park, and a buzzing nightlife. ◈ *Map A1 • www.lafayettetravel.com*

Biloxi

An hour's drive from New Orleans, this once-sleepy town has developed into the casino capital of the Gulf Coast. Today, high-rise hotels, big-name entertainers, and flashy casinos are the big draw here, not to mention the lovely beaches and exquisite homes and condominiums. The town also offers some of the best sport fishing in the region, and is famous for its delicious seafood. ◈ *www.biloxi.ms.us*

AROUND NEW ORLEANS

NEW ORLEANS' TOP 10

Left **Lafayette Cemetery** Centre **Fountain at Audubon Zoo** Right **St. Charles streetcar**

Garden District and Uptown

DEVELOPED ON FORMER PLANTATION LAND, *uptown New Orleans extends over a large part of the city and was founded by the settlers who built commercial properties and houses here. The Garden District was established on the Livaudais Plantation in 1832, where wealthy merchants, bankers, and planters built grand mansions surrounded by lush gardens, giving the area its name. This neighborhood is distinguished by its beautiful landscaping and is a relief from the urban cityscape. A great way to experience the areas is by taking a streetcar ride from the Central Business District to the top of the uptown area. A large part of the Garden District is a*

National Historic Landmark District, and visitors can explore the parks, historic buildings, and quaint antique shops of this neighborhood on foot.

Flamingoes at Audubon Zoo

🔟 Sights

1. Audubon Park
2. Audubon Zoo
3. Tulane University
4. Loyola University
5. St. Charles Streetcar
6. Toby's Corner
7. Lafayette Cemetery
8. Colonel Short's Villa
9. Briggs-Staub House
10. Robinson House

Preceding pages **Bourbon Street, Upper French Quarter**

Audubon Park

Since the late 19th century, Audubon Park has been the centerpiece of the uptown area. The land, once a sugar plantation, is now a beautifully maintained park with winding jogging paths, elegant fountains, the perfectly manicured Audubon Golf Course, and the renowned Audubon Zoo. There is also a golf clubhouse offering refreshments and lunch. The park covers a broad area, from the Mississippi River to St. Charles Avenue. Named for wildlife painter John James Audubon, the park is a favorite haunt of local bird-watchers who are likely to see egrets and several species of duck among others. ◈ 6500 Magazine St. • Map A5 • 504-861-2537 • www.auduboninstitute. org • St. Charles streetcar

Audubon Park fountain

Audubon Zoo

This New Orleans treasure is home to a massive number of animals from all over the globe and is dedicated to preserving the various species in its care. The emphasis is on interactive and hands-on exhibits, including a children's petting zoo and up-close animal-feeding experiences. Although the zoo's focus is on children's attractions, the overall experience is so enjoyable that it appeals to visitors of all age groups (see pp12–13).

Tulane University

Often called the "Harvard of the South," Tulane University is a private institution that dates back to the early 1800s. The university has been consistently ranked among the top 50 educational institutions in the U.S. and comprises ten schools, including architecture, law, liberal arts, and medicine. The university is easily identified from St. Charles Avenue by the Romanesque Gibson Hall, constructed in 1894. ◈ 6823 St. Charles Ave. • Map B5 • 504-865-5000 • www.tulane.edu • St. Charles streetcar

Loyola University

A Jesuit institution that was declared a university in 1912, Loyola University is spread over two campuses on either side of St. Charles Avenue. This is one of the largest Catholic universities in the South with nearly 3,000 students. The university offers degrees in many disciplines and is also home to the prestigious Thelonious Monk Institute of Jazz Performance. Loyola's imposing Tudor-Gothic architecture is symbolized by Marquette Hall, one of the grandest buildings on campus. ◈ 6363 St. Charles Ave. • Map B5 • 504-865-3240 • www.loyno. edu • St. Charles streetcar

Marquette Hall at Loyola University

Garden District Architecture

Three architectural styles dominate the Garden District area. Double-gallery houses are two-story structures with front-facing galleries on each level; 19th-century American town houses are narrow three-story buildings with balconies on the second floor; and the raised center-hall cottages are one-and-a-half story structures resting on brick piers.

5 St. Charles Streetcar

Streetcars are icons of New Orleans, and are as much a part of the city's character as its art and architecture. The St. Charles streetcar is the most famous. It runs for 7 miles (11 km) along St. Charles Avenue, from downtown Canal Street to uptown Carrollton Avenue, through the Central Business District. The vintage green streetcar has featured in various movies, paintings, and novels. The streetcar is the best way to get a panoramic city view, and with stops all along the long route, it enables visitors to see the city's attractions at their leisure. ◈ Map B5 • 504-827-8300 • Fare $1.25 • www.norta.com

6 Toby's Corner

A stroll through the Garden District reveals a proliferation of houses built in the Greek-Revival style. Among these is Toby's Corner, built around 1838 and believed to be the oldest house in the city. Striking in its simplicity, the house was named for Thomas Toby, a wealthy merchant originally from Philadelphia. One of the first suburban villas, the building is raised on brick piers in classic Creole style, to allow air to circulate underneath and to avoid flooding. The grounds also have an interesting fountain fashioned out of a large sugar kettle. ◈ 2340 Prytania St. • Map H5

7 Lafayette Cemetery

The above-ground tombs and vaults in the cemeteries of New Orleans are a subject of great curiosity for first-time visitors. The city is technically below sea level, so underground cemeteries cannot be managed successfully. This walled cemetery was laid out in 1833, and by 1840 it was nearly full, mostly with victims of yellow fever. Its lavish tombs are decorated in accordance with the ornate architecture of the Garden District. The best way to see the cemetery and learn about its rich history is through a guided tour, offered on Mondays, Wednesdays, Fridays, and Saturdays. ◈ 1400 Washington Ave. • Map H5 • 504-566-5011 • 7am–2:30pm Mon–Fri, 7am–12pm Sat • Adm for tours • www.lafayettecemetery.org

Above-ground tombs at Lafayette Cemetery

8 Colonel Short's Villa

Built in 1859 for Colonel Robert Short of Kentucky, this is one of the most stunning historic homes in the Garden District. Designed by architect Henry Howard, the house

Cornstalk fence at Colonel Short's Villa

is known for its cornstalk fence and is a favorite stop on walking tours. ◈ *1448 4th St.* • *Map H5*

Briggs-Staub House

The only home that retains the Gothic-Revival style in the Garden District is the Briggs-Staub House. This house was built in 1849 for Charles Briggs, who insisted that his home be referred to as a "Gothic Cottage." He commissioned architect James Gallier Sr. to design his home. The style was adhered to on the exterior, but inside, the rooms are larger and more open than one would expect to find in a typical Gothic-Revival house. ◈ *2605 Prytania St.* • *Map H5*

Robinson House

In the 1850s, indoor plumbing was a novelty in New Orleans. The Robinson House was the first house that featured "waterworks," as it was then called. Architect Henry Howard constructed a roof that served as a cistern. Gravity pushed the water down providing adequate water pressure indoors. Also unique to this home is the Italian villa-style architecture, not commonly found in the South. Another original feature of this home is the fact that the side of the house faces the street. ◈ *1415 3rd St.* • *Map H5*

A Walk Around the Garden District

Morning

It gets hot by midday in New Orleans, so start early with a stop at **Blue Plate Café** *(see p54)*, an affordably priced café serving breakfast and lunch with an assortment of unusual sandwiches. A walk up Magazine Street will offer some of the best antique shopping and galleries in the city. Stop off at the **Cole Pratt Gallery** *(see p70)*, which showcases the works of local, regional, and national artists in a beautiful minimalist space. Move on to the **Shop of the Two Sisters** *(see p70)*. This quaint and eclectic store stocks a collection of period furniture and interesting lamps and reproduction furnishings. Make sure you also take the **Garden District/ Cemetery Tour** for an informative walk around this neighborhood. You will also see the sites of several major motion-picture locations.

Afternoon

After the 2-hour tour, it will be time for lunch. Head to **Commander's Palace** *(see p71)* and be sure to try the restaurant's signature turtle soup and Creole bread pudding soufflé. After lunch, head toward St. Charles Avenue. Admire the famous **St. Charles streetcar** and take in the grand facades of the distinctive buildings on this street. Conclude your walk by early evening and step into **Emeril's Delmonico** *(see p71)* for some cocktails and a selection of the chef's small plates of the day.

Around Town – Garden District and Uptown

Left **Blue Frog Chocolates** Center **Exterior of Renaissance Shop** Right **Earthsavers**

10 Shopping

1 Blue Frog Chocolates
A chocoholic's delight, Blue Frog boasts an exotic array of individual gourmet candies, cocoa, truffles, bonbons, sauces, as well as special gift baskets and party trays. ✆ 5707 Magazine St. • Map B6 • 504-269-5707

2 Cole Pratt Gallery
This contemporary fine art gallery specializes in the works of Southern artists, which are displayed in an elegant mini-malist space. ✆ 3800 Magazine St. • Map C6 • 504-891-6789 • www.cole-prattgallery.com

3 Villa Vici
Well-known interior designer Vicki Leftwich offers innovative lighting, avant-garde furniture, and fine fabrics at her store. This is a one-stop shop for home decor. ✆ 2930 Magazine St. • Map H6 • 504-899-2931

4 Shop of the Two Sisters
Sisters Lee and Rose Ali offer interesting and unusual lamps, intricately detailed period chairs, decorative pieces, reproduction furnishings, and more in their rather offbeat store. ✆ 1800 Magazine St. • Map J5 • 504-525-2747

5 Renaissance Shop
Fine antique reproductions, expert upholstery, and meticulous furniture repair is this shop's forte. ✆ 2104 Magazine St. • Map J5 • 504-525-8568

6 Belladonna Day Spa and Retail Therapy
This two-story space houses an elegant personal-care and home accessories store on the ground floor and a world-class spa upstairs. ✆ 2900 Magazine St. • Map H6 • 504-891-4393

7 Mignon Faget, Ltd.
For over 40 years, Mignon Faget, an upscale designer jewelry store, has created beautiful custom-created and specially handcrafted pieces. ✆ 3801 Magazine St. • Map C6 • 504-891-2005

8 Perlis
Since 1939, Perlis has been the clothier of choice for many New Orleans families. The store offers casual wear for men, women, and children. It also has a rental and sales division for formal wear. ✆ 6070 Magazine St. • Map B6 • 504-895-8661

9 Weinstein's, Inc.
Weinstein's stocks fine European fashion items for women and an array of upscale designer brands for both men and women. ✆ 4011 Magazine St. • Map C6 • 504-895-6278

10 Earthsavers
This pleasant-smelling shop has aromatherapy and day-spa facilities, along with a collection of personal-care and gift items. ✆ 5501 Magazine St. • Map B6 • 504-899-8555

Price Categories

For a three-course meal for one, with half a bottle of wine (or equivalent meal), taxes, and extra charges.

$	under $25
$$	$25–$40
$$$	$40–$55
$$$$	$55–$70
$$$$$	over $70

Above **The chic interior of Coquette**

Places to Eat

1 Lilette
Chef and owner John Harris has created an intimate, fine-dining experience offering authentic and elegant French-Italian cuisine. Try their irresistible roasted Muscovy duck breast. ⬙ 3637 Magazine St. • Map C6 • 504-895-1636 • $$$$

2 Commander's Palace
This is the *grande dame* of New Orleans fine dining. Creole cuisine at its very best.
⬙ 1403 Washington Ave. • Map H5 • 504-899-8221 • $$$$$

3 Upperline Restaurant
A massive art collection is on display here. Do not miss the sensational fried green tomatoes with shrimp rémoulade. ⬙ 1413 Upperline St. • Map C6 • 504-891-9822 • $$$

4 Coquette
One of the newer entrants in the local dining scene, Coquette looks like a chic Parisian bistro. All menu items are offered in both small plate and entrée size. Their roasted oysters and pork-belly rillettes are excellent.
⬙ 2800 Magazine St. • Map H6 • 504-265-0421 • $$$

5 Emeril's Delmonico
This is the most upscale of Emeril's chain of restaurants. Diners can try Chef Spencer Minch's creative global cuisine. ⬙ 1300 St. Charles Ave. • Map R2 • 504-525-4937 • $$$$$

6 Martinique
Surrounding a courtyard, this charming bistro serves experimental French cuisine. The pork tenderloin with pear chutney, blue cheese, and a port demi-glace is a must-try.
⬙ 5908 Magazine St. • Map B6 • 504-891-8495 • $$$$

7 Dante's Kitchen
This place serves hearty American food with a touch of the South. Remember to try the rabbit cassoulet. ⬙ 736 Dante St. • Map A4 • 504-861-3121 • $$$

8 Pascal's Manale
The barbecued shrimp, an iconic local favorite, was invented at Pascal's Manale nearly a century ago. Today, this restaurant still uses the same recipe, and offers seafood and Italian specialties. ⬙ 1838 Napoleon Ave. • Map C5 • 504-895-4877 • $$$

9 Dick and Jenny's
Home-cooked meals and luscious calorific desserts, such as the chocolate pecan chess pie, are the specialties of this place. ⬙ 4501 Tchoupitoulas St. • Map C6 • 504-894-9880 • $$

10 Gautreau's
Tucked away in a small garden in an uptown neighborhood, Gautreau's offers classic New Orleans cuisine in a delightful fine-dining atmosphere. ⬙ 1728 Sonia St. • Map B5 • 504-899-7397 • $$$

Around Town – Garden District and Uptown

Recommend your favorite restaurant on **traveldk.com**

Left **Sign, Harrah's Casino** Center **Aquarium of the Americas** Right **Exhibit, Audubon Insectarium**

CBD and Warehouse District

THE GENERAL HUSTLE AND BUSTLE THAT *surrounds daily activity in the downtown area extends all the way through the Warehouse and Central Business Districts. Like any other major American city, downtown is a hub of commerce, entertainment, dining, and shopping. What distinguishes New Orleans' downtown area is the large concentration of citizens who live here,* as well as the number of historic buildings dating back to the 19th century, which exist in between the profusion of newer structures. Today, many of the old warehouses in this neighborhood have been converted into stylish spaces housing jazz bars, restaurants, hotels, galleries, and museums.

🔟 Sights

1 Aquarium of the Americas
2 Harrah's New Orleans Casino
3 The National World War II Museum
4 Ogden Museum of Southern Art
5 Mercedes-Benz Superdome
6 Audubon Insectarium
7 Contemporary Arts Center
8 Canal Street
9 Julia Street
10 Spanish Plaza

Restaurants and skyscrapers towering over Spanish Plaza

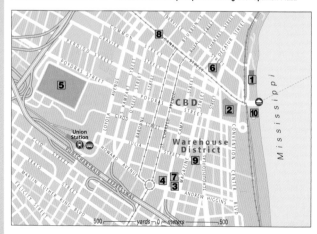

Aquarium of the Americas

Opened to the public in 1990, this aquarium is held to be the finest of its kind in the country. Housed in an ultra-modern building, the Aquarium of the Americas is located on the banks of the Mississippi. It has three levels of fascinating displays of live creatures that inhabit the sea. From the entertaining penguin colony to the huge array of sharks and walk-through underwater tunnel, the Aquarium appeals to visitors of all ages. On arrival, be sure to check out the timing of animal feedings for that day (see pp18–19).

Harrah's New Orleans Casino

A grand casino covering an area of 115,000 sq ft (10,684 sq m), Harrah's tempts visitors with a variety of entertainment options ranging from gambling to fine dining. The casino boasts more than 2,000 slot machines, and table games such as roulette, baccarat, and poker, on more than 100 tables, making it a haven for gamers. As well as this, the casino houses the upscale Besh Steak House, a stylish cocktail lounge called Masquerade with an ice bar, a lavish buffet restaurant, and several smaller specialty restaurants (see p30).

Colorful corals at Aquarium of the Americas

The National World War II Museum

Boasting a large collection of American World War II memorabilia, this museum was created with the purpose of honoring the 16 million Americans who contributed to the war effort. Do not miss the "Behind the Lines Tour," a fascinating visit to the museum's vault with a curator. ⊗ 945 Magazine St. • Map Q3 • 504-528-1944 • 9am–5pm daily • Adm • www.nationalww2museum.org

Ogden Museum of Southern Art

A substantial part of Roger Ogden's huge collection of Southern art was donated to create this museum. The multi-level building has an industrial feel about it and houses the finest and most diverse collection of Southern art in the U.S., featuring everything from folk art to contemporary pieces. ⊗ 925 Camp St. • Map Q3 • 504-539-9600 • 10am–5pm Wed–Mon, 6–8pm Thu • Adm • www.ogdenmuseum.org

Sculpture and paintings on display, Ogden Museum of Southern Art

Exhibit in the Audubon Insectarium

5 Mercedes-Benz Superdome

A distinct saucer-shaped landmark, the Mercedes-Benz Superdome is home to the local football team, the Saints. However, this facility is much more than just a sports venue: it hosts conventions, exhibitions, car shows, and rock concerts. The Superdome covers more than 13 acres (5 ha) and seats more than 70,000 people. It has been the site of 9 NFL (National Football League) championships as well as an American presidential convention. ◈ *Sugarbowl Drive • Map N1 • 504-587-3663 • Call for timings • Adm • www.superdome.com*

6 Audubon Insectarium

The city's old U.S. Custom House, on the edge of the French Quarter, has been artfully transformed into a museum devoted to all kinds of bugs. Visitors are treated to "up-close and personal" live insect encounters. You can experience being shrunk to insect size when surrounded by the huge exhibits in the Life Underground display, discover the mating and reproduction cycles of insects in the Metamorphosis exhibit, journey through the Louisiana Swamp, or enjoy the tranquility of an Asian-inspired butterfly garden and watch hundreds of the winged creatures flit about. Do not miss the cutting-edge insect cuisine. The less intrepid visitor can enjoy an ordinary burger at the Tiny Termite Café with bug-inspired decor *(see p31)*.

7 Contemporary Arts Center

Formed in 1976, by a group of artists as a project to bring together the visual and performing arts, the Contemporary Arts Center (CAC) was one of the earliest art addresses in the Warehouse District. It is housed in a cavernous building, which has been refashioned into a workspace for artists, exhibitions, and theater. Although the focus is on visual arts, educational programs and performing arts run a close second. ◈ *900 Camp St • Map Q3 • 504 5283805 • 11am–4pm Wed–Sun • Adm • www.cacno.org*

Dome roof of Mercedes-Benz Superdome

Canal Street

8 This historic road originally divided old New Orleans into the French and American parts. Canal Street, whose name derives from a proposed canal in that area which was never built, is the main boulevard in the downtown area. The most in-demand spot to watch the Mardi Gras parade, it is lined with restaurants, boutiques, and luxury hotels. The Canal streetcar is a good way to explore the sights along the length of this road *(see pp30–31)*.

Canal streetcar

Julia Street

9 One of the main streets in the Warehouse District, Julia Street features some of the city's most appealing historic architecture and is New Orleans' gallery neighborhood. An annual street party – White Linen Night – is hosted here in August, when people can browse through art, eat and drink, and enjoy live music though the night. ⊗ *Map Q3*

Spanish Plaza

10 Located on the edge of the Mississippi Riverfront, the Spanish Plaza with its large central fountain and colorful tiles is a place where visitors can relax and enjoy a view of the river. It is also the starting point for the Creole Queen cruise and hosts outdoor concerts and parties *(see p20)*.

A Walk Around the Warehouse District

Morning

🕐 Begin your day with a hearty breakfast of poached eggs, crab cakes, fried green tomatoes, and strong coffee at **7 on Fulton** *(see p79)*, on Convention Center Boulevard, and then make your way to the **Woldenberg Riverfront Park** *(see p20)*, a lovely green area with contemporary sculpture and a view of the river. Just past the park is the **Aquarium of the Americas** *(see pp18–19)*, which is fun to explore. Walk a few blocks to **Julia Street** to see its quaint architecture and plethora of art galleries. Stop by at the nationally acclaimed **Arthur Roger Gallery** *(see p77)*, the pinnacle of the local arts scene. Along the way, shop at the many boutiques before making your way to the **National World War II Museum** *(see p73)* to see its collection of war memorabilia. Treat yourself to a tasty lunch at **Sun Ray Grill** *(see p79)*.

Afternoon

After lunch walk around the corner to the **Contemporary Arts Center** and the **Ogden Museum of Southern Art** *(see p73)* for more visual stimuli and some fantastic pieces of art. End a day of art and culture at **Tommy's Cuisine** *(see p79)*. Check out its Creole delicacies and great collection of wines. Later, make your way back to the Mississippi Riverfront to end your day with one of New Orleans' spectacular sunsets.

Left **Woldenberg Riverfront Park** Center **Algiers Ferry** Right **Preservation Resource Center**

Best of the Rest

1 Loa
Popular with visitors and locals, Loa is a shadowy, voodoo-themed bar in the International House Hotel *(see p119)*. It offers boutique wines and an array of cocktails. ✆ 221 Camp St. • Map N3 • 504–553-9550 • www.ihhotel.com

2 Louisiana Children's Museum
The displays here are interactive and educational with monthly special events and visiting exhibits. ✆ 420 Julia St. • Map Q4 • 504-523-1357 • 9:30am–5pm Mon–Sat, noon–5pm Sun • www.lcm.org

3 Woldenberg Riverfront Park
This lovely green area along the banks of the Mississippi River is perfect for biking, jogging, or just spending a lazy afternoon. The park hosts festivals and events through the year *(see p20)*.

4 The World Trade Center
An imposing structure overlooking the Mississippi, the World Trade Center is the city's hub for international trade *(see p30)*.

5 St. Patrick's Church
Located in the middle of the Central Business District, this Gothic-style church is a National Historic Landmark and an elegant reminder of old New Orleans. ✆ 724 Camp St. • Map P3 • 504-525-4413 • Timings vary • www.oldstpatricks.org

6 Masquerade at Harrah's New Orleans Casino
A 32-ft (10-m) ice bar and 42-ft (13-m) media tower are the chief attractions of this chic nightclub in Harrah's Casino. There is a live jazz happy hour every Thursday from 6pm onward *(see p30)*.

7 Ernest N. Morial Convention Center
One of the largest convention centers in the country, this building has state-of-the-art technology *(see p21)*.

8 Mulate's Cajun Restaurant and Dance Hall
This restaurant is known for its authentic Cajun food and lively Cajun music. Dancing lessons are offered for first timers. Do not miss the excellent crabmeat *au gratin.* ✆ 201 Julia St. • Map Q4 • 504-522-1492

9 Preservation Resource Center
This nonprofit organization aims to preserve the historic neighborhoods and develop the resources of the city. ✆ 923 Tchoupitoulas St. • Map Q3 • 504-581-7032 • 9am–5pm Mon–Fri • www.prcno.org

10 Algiers Ferry
Visitors can take a ferry ride to experience the city from the river. This ferry starts from the foot of Canal Street and ends at the historic Algiers Point. ✆ Map P5 • 6am–midnight • Adm from Algiers point; free from Canal St.

Left **Paintings at the Arthur Roger Gallery** Right **Exhibit at the Contemporary Arts Center**

TOP 10 Warehouse District Galleries

Arthur Roger Gallery
Established in 1978 by Arthur Roger, who is a world-famous purveyor of fine art, this gallery is one of the most high-profile art spaces in the city.
◎ 432/434 Julia St. • Map Q3 • 504-522-1999 • www.arthurrogergallery.com

George Schmidt Gallery
The New Orleans artist George Schmidt is known for his pieces documenting the history of New Orleans. This gallery exclusively showcases his work.
◎ 626 Julia St. • Map Q3 • 504-592-0206 • 12:30–4:30pm Tue–Sat • www.georgeschmidt.com

Le Mieux Galleries
Artists from Louisiana and the rest of the Gulf Coast are the focal point of this gallery. ◎ 332 Julia St. • Map Q4 • 504-522-5988 • 10am–6pm Mon–Sat • www.lemieuxgalleries.com

Jean Bragg Gallery of Southern Art
The focus here is on Southern art, especially landscape and architectural subjects. ◎ 600 Julia St. • Map Q3 • 504-895-7375 • 10am–5pm Mon–Sat • www.jeanbragg.com

Steve Martin Fine Art
Originally designed as an artist's workspace, this gallery has gained international recognition and displays works across genres. ◎ 624 Julia St. • Map Q3 • 504-566-1390 • 10am–6pm daily • www.stevemartinfineart.com

Heriard-Cimino Gallery
This gallery showcases abstract, figurative, and conceptual work by established artists from New York and Miami. Works of art displayed here include paintings, photography, and installations. ◎ 440 Julia St. • Map Q3 • 504-525-7300 • 10am–5pm Tue–Sat • www.heriard-cimino.com

New Orleans ArtWorks
This gallery has two working studios in the back. One is dedicated to glass art, while the other is for print-making. ◎ 727 Magazine St. • Map P3 • 504-529-7279 • 10am–5pm Mon–Fri • www.neworleans-glassworks.com

Contemporary Arts Center
The CAC dedicates itself to cutting-edge, even experimental art. Local and national artists exhibit here *(see p74)*.

d.o.c.s. Gallery
The ambitious gallery owners at d.o.c.s. mount new shows every month, featuring the work of two artists each time. The gallery specializes in contemporary works. ◎ 709 Camp St. • Map P3 • 504-524-3936 • 11am–5pm Tue–Sat • www.docsgallery.com

Jonathan Ferrara Gallery
This gallery features contemporary works by regional and international artists, as well as new talent. ◎ 400 Julia St. • Map Q4 • 504-522-5471 • 11am–5pm Mon–Sat • www.jonathanferraragallery.com

For more on art galleries in New Orleans **See pp36–7.**

Left **Exterior, Adler's Jewelry** Center **Hats at Meyer the Hatter** Right **Riverwalk Marketplace**

TOP 10 Places to Shop

1 Rubensteins
Owned by the same family since 1924, Rubensteins is regarded as the finest men's clothing store in the city. It has also started stocking stylish womenswear *(see p31)*.

2 Shops at Canal Place
A luxury hotel, theaters, and a three-level shopping center with several upscale boutiques makes up the Canal Place complex *(see p30)*.

3 Adler's Jewelry
Considered one of the finest jewelry retailers in town, Adler's is famous for custom-designed jewelry. ✪ *722 Canal St. • Map M3 • 504-523-5292*

4 Shops at the Ritz-Carlton, New Orleans
The ground floor at the Ritz-Carlton New Orleans covers 25,000 sq ft (2,300 sq m) and houses a number of high-end stores and a luxury spa *(see p30)*.

5 Riverwalk Marketplace
Located on the edge of the Mississippi, the Riverwalk Marketplace houses shops, galleries, bars, restaurants, and other entertainment venues under the same roof *(see p21)*.

6 Jack Sutton Fine Jewelry
Elegant jewelry, ready-to-wear designs, and custom pieces are on offer here. ✪ *365 Canal St. • Map N4 • 504-522-8080*

7 Ann Taylor
Featuring classic American designs for women, Ann Taylor stores offer mix-and-match separates, accessories, and shoes, as well as gifts. ✪ *333 Canal St. • Map N4 • 504-529-2306*

8 Meyer the Hatter
Meyer features fine quality headwear for men in classic, contemporary, and trendy designs. ✪ *120 St. Charles Ave. • Map N3 • 504-525-1048*

9 Saks Fifth Avenue
Considered one of the most upscale retailers in the country, Saks Fifth Avenue offers an extensive range of designer products and holds its own with the best department stores in the country. ✪ *301 Canal St. • Map N4 • 504-524-2200*

10 Brooks Brothers
For decades, Brooks Brothers has provided fine formal and upscale casual attire for men. The New Orleans branch of the store is located on the ground floor of The Shops at Canal Place *(see p30)*.

Around Town – CBD and Warehouse District

Price Categories

For a three-course meal for one, with half a bottle of wine (or equivalent meal), taxes, and extra charges.

$	under $25
$$	$25–$40
$$$	$40–$55
$$$$	$55–$70
$$$$$	over $70

Above **Stylish interiors at Emeril's**

TOP 10 Places to Eat

1 Palace Café
Housed in a 19th-century building, Palace Café serves seafood and Creole specialties. Their white chocolate bread pudding is excellent. ⑨ *605 Canal St. • Map N3 • 504-523-1661 • $$$$*

2 La Cote Brasserie
This chic restaurant is known for its Southern specialties such as the char-grilled lobster tails and vanilla sourdough French toast. ⑨ *700 Tchoupitoulas St. • Map P4 • 504-613-2350 • $$$$*

3 Herbsaint
Named for the famous anise-flavored liqueur, this eatery features Southern classics like grits (thick maize porridge) and dark roux gumbos (seafood soup flavored with a brown sauce). ⑨ *701 St. Charles Ave. • Map P3 • 504-524-4114 • $$$$$ • Closed Sun*

4 Tommy's Cuisine
Specializing in classic Creole and Italian dishes, Tommy's makes a delicious rosemary chicken. ⑨ *746 Tchoupitoulas St. • Map Q4 • 504-581-1103 • $$$$$ • Closed L*

5 Café Adelaide
This upscale and artsy fine-dining restaurant excels in Creole dishes. Try their praline-crusted pork tenderloin. ⑨ *300 Poydras St. • Map P4 • 504-595-3305 • $$$$*

6 Gordon Biersch
This brewery-cum-restaurant has a popular happy hour. Its brewery tours and beer samplings make it a favorite among visitors and locals alike. ⑨ *200 Poydras St. • Map P4 • 504-552-2739 • $$$*

7 Emeril's
Named for its famous chef, Emeril Lagasse, this restaurant boasts a diverse menu including *paneed* (coated in bread crumbs) veal and crispy sweetbreads. ⑨ *800 Tchoupitoulas St. • Map Q4 • 504-528-9393 • $$$$$*

8 Sun Ray Grill
A bright eatery serving international cuisine featuring eclectic dishes such as Santa Fe burrito and guava-glazed duck. ⑨ *1051 Annunciation St. • Map R3 • 504-566-0021 • $$$*

9 7 on Fulton
A spacious dining room and bar, 7 on Fulton serves culinary delights such as alligator ravioli. ⑨ *701 Convention Center Blvd. • Map Q4 • 504-525-7555 • $$$$*

10 Wolfe's in the Warehouse
Wolfe's Creole-French cooking tempts with its bread-crumbed redfish and pan-roasted duck sausage. ⑨ *859 Convention Center Blvd. • Map Q4 • 504-613-2882 • $$$$$*

Around Town – CBD and Warehouse District

Left **Pitot House Museum** Center **Houses along Bayou St. John** Right **Angelo Brocato's shop**

Mid-City

EXTENDING FROM THE FRENCH QUARTER *toward Lake Pontchartrain,* Mid-City was carved out of a former plantation and is the greenest part of New Orleans. Dominated by the New Orleans City Park and intersected by the major thoroughfares of Canal Street and Esplanade Avenue, Mid-City is a predominantly residential area and is home to the original New Orleans families. Their distinct culture is exemplified by the fact that they have had their own Mardi Gras krewes since 1933. The Canal streetcar winds its way through this lovely neighborhood, which is dotted with cemeteries, canals, parkways, and Creole mansions. Although the area was heavily damaged by Hurricane Katrina, extensive reconstruction work has restored much of its original charm.

Canal streetcar

Sights

1. New Orleans Museum of Art
2. New Orleans City Park
3. New Orleans Botanical Gardens
4. Degas House
5. Fair Grounds Race Course & Slots
6. Bayou St. John
7. Angelo Brocato's Ice Cream & Confectionery
8. The Sydney and Walda Besthoff Sculpture Garden
9. Pitot House Museum
10. Canal Streetcar

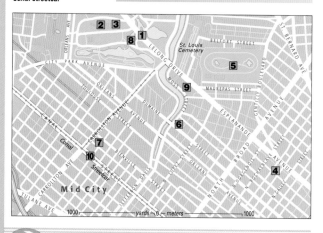

1 New Orleans Museum of Art

An architectural and cultural gem in the Mid-City area, the New Orleans Museum of Art (NOMA), showcases 10 permanent collections from all over the world, as well as high-profile rotating exhibitions. NOMA also has an active schedule of educational programs, children's programs, and special events which are open to the public. The museum gift shop offers some high-end and unique works of art, jewelry, accessories, and books *(see pp8–11)*.

2 New Orleans City Park

Spanning 1,300 acres (513 ha), New Orleans City Park is one of the largest urban parks in the country, with a variety of gardens, sculptures, buildings, and activities. Attractions such as Storyland and the Carousel Gardens Amusement Park *(see p26)* make this is a great spot for children. For visitors interested in outdoor activities, there are waterways for canoeing, tennis courts, and golf courses. The city park also includes the New Orleans Botanical Gardens and hosts concerts, festivals, garden shows, holiday light

Carefully restored interior of Degas House

Gift shop at NOMA

spectaculars, fundraisers, weddings and other private events *(see pp26–7)*.

3 New Orleans Botanical Gardens

Originally known as the City Park Rose Garden, these gardens opened in 1936, combining landscaping techniques with art and architecture. Today, more than 2,000 plant varieties can be found here. Mostly cared for by volunteers, the gardens feature plants and flowers indigenous to Louisiana. Because of the tropical climate in New Orleans, the growing season lasts most of the year, allowing the Botanical Gardens to showcase its best foliage and flowering plants almost year round. The adjacent conservatory features a simulated tropical rain forest and a raging waterfall *(see p26)*.

4 Degas House

Edgar Degas, the renowned French Impressionist painter, lived in this house in 1872–3, and created at least 22 works of art during this period. Today, the house is considered one of the finest bed and breakfast inns in the city. There is a Degas Tour which explores the life of the artist during the Reconstruction Era (period after the Civil War). ⓢ *2306 Esplanade Ave. • Map E2 • 504-821-5009 • Tours by appointment • Adm • www.degashouse.com*

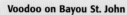

Angelo Brocato's Ice Cream & Confectionery

Fair Grounds Race Course & Slots

Well over 100 years old, the Fair Grounds are home to the third-oldest continuously running race track in the country as well as over 600 slot machines. The annual races are held from Thanksgiving Day to the end of March. Visitors can watch the races outdoors, or enjoy the comforts of the clubhouse, with fine dining and monitors to keep abreast of events on the track. Fair Grounds also hosts the New Orleans Jazz and Heritage Festival *(see p60).* ⬥ *1751 Gentilly Blvd. • Map D1 • 504-944-5515 • Adm for clubhouse • www.fairgroundsracecourse.com*

Bayou St. John

One of the most picturesque parts of Mid-City is Bayou St. John, an inner-city creek that separates two residential neighborhoods. Visitors can explore the area on foot or on a bicycle. The bayou is famous for having been the site of voodoo rituals in the 18th and 19th centuries. ⬥ *Map J2*

Angelo Brocato's Ice Cream & Confectionery

Angelo Brocato's has managed to retain its quality since opening in 1905. This charming old-world shop, run by the third generation of Brocatos, has a friendly staff. Italian specialties such as *gelato* (low-fat ice cream), *spumoni* (molded Italian ice cream) and *torrone* (Italian nougat) continue to attract the masses. ⬥ *214 N. Carrollton Ave. • Map C2 • 504-486-1465*

The Sydney & Walda Besthoff Sculpture Garden

Named after prominent art collectors and patrons, the Besthoffs, this garden includes a collection of contemporary sculpture from across the world. The pieces, donated by the Besthoff Foundation, are displayed among the ancient oaks, magnolias, and tranquil lagoons in this exquisite garden, which is adjacent to the musuem. A free cell-phone tour with information on the sculptures is available *(see pp8, 11).*

Picturesque stretch around Bayou St. John

Pitot House Museum

Over two centuries old, Pitot House is a Creole-Colonial style building located on the banks of the Bayou St. John. It has had several owners, including lawyers and nuns, but is named for James Pitot, the first American mayor of New Orleans, who lived here from 1810 to 1819. It was beautifully restored by the Louisiana Landmarks Society in the 1960s, and is now a museum and a National Trust for Historic Preservation Partner Place. Organized tours are offered in the museum and its sprawling, elegant gardens. ⊗ *1440 Moss St. • Map J3 • 504-482-0312 • Tours 10am–3pm Wed–Fri, Saturdays by appointment only • Adm • www.pitothouse.org*

The Pitot House Museum

Canal Streetcar

This line, which begins at the Mississippi River, dates back to the mid-19th century. It travels through the CBD and well into Mid-City before coming to a stop at NOMA *(see pp8–11)*. The New Orleans streetcar is iconic to the city. These vintage vehicles are fitted with wooden seats and painted a bright red. Locals use the streetcars as an inexpensive way to commute, whereas visitors find it the best mode of sightseeing, as the streetcar stops at most of the significant sights in Mid-City and travels at a leisurely pace. ⊗ *504-248-3900 • Adm • www.norta.com*

A Tour of New Orleans City Park

Morning

🕐 Hop on to the Canal streetcar from the French Quarter or downtown area for a scenic ride into Mid-City. The last stop is the **New Orleans Museum of Art** *(see pp8–11)*, where you can get off and explore the museum, as well as walk along handsomely sculptured lawns and flower gardens, under centuries-old oaks at the **New Orleans City Park** *(see pp26–7)*. This will work up an appetite, so treat yourself to a lavish meal at **Ralph's on the Park** *(see p85)*, which is famous for innovative Creole food as well as its fantastic location.

Afternoon

After lunch, walk around the beautifully designed **Sydney & Walda Besthoff Sculpture Garden**. Then make your way to the **New Orleans Botanical Gardens** *(see p26)*, where you can view the miniature **Train Garden** *(see p27)* and also enjoy a walk through the adjacent conservatory and theme gardens. Along the way, be sure to make a stop at **Storyland** *(see p26)*, a delightful place for people of all ages and a special treat for children. From here, walk over to the nearby **Carousel Gardens Amusement Park** *(see p27)*, which houses one of the few remaining antique wooden carousels in the country. Do stop by NOLA City Bark, New Orleans' first officially designated dog park. End with a delicious *gelato* in one of the many flavors available at **Angelo Brocato's Ice Cream & Confectionery**.

Left **Shotgun-style cottages** Center **Pandora's Snowballs sign** Right **Dueling Oaks**

🔟 Neighborhood Attractions

1 Shotgun-Style Cottages
These narrow rectangular houses, or "shotguns," have rooms built directly behind each other. The name derives from the fact that if a shotgun was fired, the bullet would go straight through the whole house.

2 American Can Company
A manufacturing plant converted into an upscale condominium complex, the American Can Company is a prestigious Mid-City address with restaurants and a fashionable shopping area. ⓢ *3700 Orleans Ave.* • *Map H3* • *504-207-0090* • *www.americancanapts.com*

3 Jefferson Davis Monument
This stone statue is dedicated to Jefferson Davis, President of the Confederate States during the American Civil War. ⓢ *Jefferson Davis Parkway* • *Map C2*

4 Mid-City Art Market
On the last Saturday of each month, local artists and craftsmen display and sell their wares at makeshift stalls in this market in Palmer Park. ⓢ *Carrollton Ave.* • *Map B3* • *10am–4pm*

5 Willie Mae's Scotch House
Supposedly serving the best fried chicken in the city, Willie Mae's Scotch House has been a very popular eatery since World War II. ⓢ *2401 St. Ann St.* • *Map E2* • *504-822-9503* • *11am–3pm Mon–Sat*

6 Banks Street Bar & Grill
Little neighborhood cafés and bars dot the city, and Banks Street Bar & Grill is one such spot. It offers some of the best local food and great live music almost every night. ⓢ *4401 Banks St.* • *Map C2* • *504-486-0258*

7 Pandora's Snowballs
A popular local hangout, Pandora's Snowballs is a small corner shop offering cups of shaved ice in a variety of flavors as well as creamy soft-serve ice creams. A perfect way to beat the heat. ⓢ *901 N. Carrollton Ave.* • *Map H3*

8 Dueling Oaks
These massive overhanging oak trees in New Orleans City Park served as a backdrop for countless duels in the early 1800s. ⓢ *Map H2*

9 The Train Garden
This miniature authentic replica of the city of New Orleans is located inside the Botanical Gardens *(see p26)*. It is complete with a fully operating train and buildings made out of natural materials *(see p27)*.

10 Dillard University
This liberal-arts college was established in 1869 to educate the newly freed African-Americans. Today, the school offers 34 majors in six academic disciplines. ⓢ *2601 Gentilly Blvd.* • *504-283-8822* • *www.dillard.edu*

Price Categories

For a three-course meal for one, with half a bottle of wine (or equivalent meal), taxes, and extra charges.

$	under $25
$$	$25–$40
$$$	$40–$55
$$$$	$55–$70
$$$$$	over $70

Above **Cozy interiors at Café Degas**

🔟 Dining in Mid-City

1 Crescent City Steak House
The steaks at this dining room are outstanding. Curtains enclose the private booths. ⌾ *1001 N. Broad St. • Map D2 • 504-821-3271 • Closed Mon • $$$$*

2 Parkway Bakery & Tavern
This quaint shop serves some of the best fried shrimp po'boys *(see p51)* and roast beef sandwiches in the city. ⌾ *538 Hagan Ave. • Map D2 • 866-755-9842 • $*

3 Café Minh
Renowned for its French-Vietnamese fusion cuisine, Café Minh's specials include coconut shrimp and sweet corn soup. ⌾ *4139 Canal St. • Map C2 • 504-482-6266 • Closed Sun • $$$*

4 Café Degas
Named for Edgar Degas, this tiny French bistro excels in light, subtle dishes. ⌾ *3127 Esplanade Ave. • Map D2 • 504-945-5635 • Closed Mon–Tue • $$$*

5 Mandina's Restaurant
A local institution, Mandina's serves traditional delicacies such as jambalaya and a hearty gumbo *(see p51)*. ⌾ *3800 Canal St. • Map C2 • 504-482-9179 • $$$*

6 Venezia
A favorite among locals, Venezia has a basic ambience, but the food is spicy and authentically Italian. ⌾ *134 North Carrollton Ave. • Map C2 • 504-488-7991 • Closed Mon–Tue • $$*

7 Liuzza's
Famous for its lasagna and huge, icy "fishbowls" of draft beer, Liuzza's is a tightly packed and friendly neighborhood diner. ⌾ *3636 Bienville St. • Map C2 • 504-482-9120 • Closed Sun–Mon • $$*

8 Dooky Chase
Run by legendary chef Leah Chase who is famous for her "Creole Soul" food, Dooky Chase is authentic and has all the warmth of home cooking. ⌾ *2301 Orleans Ave. • Map E3 • 504-821-0600 • Closed Sat–Mon • $$$*

9 Lola's
This popular Spanish restaurant allows patrons to bring their own wine. Do try their fantastic and large portion of seafood paella. ⌾ *3312 Esplanade Ave. • Map D2 • 504-488-6946 • $$$*

10 Ralph's on the Park
This stellar restaurant, run by Ralph Brennan, features innovative Creole cuisine. The excellent tabasco and honey-glazed flounder is a must-try. ⌾ *900 City Park Ave. • Map G2 • 504-488-1000 • Closed L • $$$$$*

Recommend your favorite restaurant on **traveldk.com**

Left **Window detail, Old Ursuline Convent** Center **Congo Square** Right **Esplanade Avenue**

Lower French Quarter, Marigny, and Treme

THE PART OF THE FRENCH QUARTER *farthest from the CBD is referred to as the Lower French Quarter. Exploring this lively area, visitors may pass some "notorious" parts, before reaching great restaurants and bars, as well as tiny boutiques selling everything from vintage clothing to hard-to-find antiques. The best way to see this area is on foot. Wander into Faubourg Marigny, across from the French Quarter, and then into Faubourg Treme, the oldest African-American neighborhood in the country. In the Marigny, the biggest attraction is Frenchmen Street with its bohemian nightclubs, while Treme is home to some of the oldest architecture in the city.*

Vintage shop, Decatur Street

🔟 Sights

1. Mahalia Jackson Theater of the Performing Arts
2. Old Ursuline Convent
3. Armstrong Park
4. Congo Square
5. Washington Square
6. New Orleans Jazz National Historical Park
7. Esplanade Avenue
8. Soniat House
9. Lower Decatur Street
10. The French Market

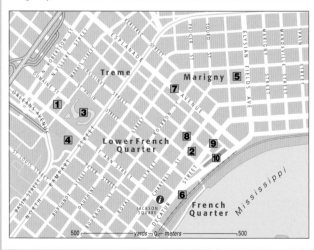

Preceding pages **St. Louis Cathedral, Upper French Quarter**

1 Mahalia Jackson Theater of the Performing Arts

Named for the internationally acclaimed Queen of Gospel Music, Mahalia Jackson, this world-class theater showcases Broadway musicals and diverse performances by famous musicians, comedians, dancers, ballet companies, and much more. This multi-level theater is the highlight of Basin Street and can seat 2,100 people. ◙ 1419 Basin St. • Map K3 • 504-287-0351 • Call for timings • Adm • www.mahaliajacksontheater.com

2 Old Ursuline Convent

Built in 1752, the Old Ursuline Convent is the oldest surviving building in the Mississippi River Valley. Attached to a Catholic church, the convent was home to the founding Ursuline Sisters. Tours of the convent reveal its beautiful hand-crafted cypress staircase, paintings, religious statuary, and bronze busts. The building has operated as an orphanage, a hospital, and a residence hall for bishops. ◙ 1100 Chartres St. • Map L5 • 504-529-3040 • Tours: 10am, 11am, 1pm, 2pm, 3pm Tue–Fri; 11:15am, 1pm, and 2pm Sat–Sun • Adm

Grand facade, Old Ursuline Convent

Archway at the entrance to Armstrong Park

3 Armstrong Park

Directly across from the French Quarter, the lush 32-acre (13-ha) Armstrong Park winds around the Mahalia Jackson Theater with its extensive green spaces and waterways. At the entrance to the park is a majestic statue of Louis "Satchmo" Armstrong, one of New Orleans' favorite sons, and a world-famous jazz musician. At various times throughout the year, Armstrong Park is the site of organized jazz concerts and festivals, and the starting point for the "Krewe of Barkus" dog parade during Mardi Gras. ◙ 835 North Rampart St. • Map K4 • 504-286-2100

4 Congo Square

Located right in the heart of Armstrong Park, Congo Square is the place where slaves and free people of color gathered throughout the 19th century for meetings, open markets, and the African dance and drumming celebrations that played a major role in the development of jazz. Local voodoo practitioners still consider Congo Square a spiritual base and gather here for important rituals. The history of Congo Square is occasionally celebrated with free Sunday afternoon concerts and public gatherings. ◙ 835 North Rampart St. • Map L3 • 504-286-2100

Faubourg *is the French term for suburb.*

Red brick facade, Soniat House

5 Washington Square

Originally a huge plantation, Faubourg Marigny today forms a significant neighborhood in the city. Right in the center of this area is Washington Square, an urban park that is the site for special events and festivals. The most important of these is the annual Gay Pride Festival. Washington Square is a great place for a walk or a meal at any of the numerous surrounding restaurants. ◉ Map K6

6 New Orleans Jazz National Historical Park

The U.S. National Park Service designated a 4-acre (2-ha) site within Armstrong Park as the New Orleans Jazz National Historical Park. The idea was to honor jazz, considered America's original musical art form, and to commemorate the city of New Orleans as the birthplace of jazz. This park is home to Perseverence Hall, a building constructed in 1819, where African-American musicians trained and performed

for both African-American and white audiences. Many of the original jazz halls were demolished, but this one was saved and placed on the National Register of Historic Places. ◉ *916 N. Peters St.* • *Map L5* • *504-589-4841* • *9am–5pm Tue–Sat* • *www.nps.gov*

7 Esplanade Avenue

One of the most picturesque streets in the city, Esplanade Avenue stretches from the Mississippi River to New Orleans City Park. This road separates the French Quarter from the Faubourg Marigny. It is lined with lovely historical mansions dating back to the 19th century as it was the address of choice for rich Creole citizens. There are also several quaint bistros, cafés, ethnic restaurants, and houses representing most of the architectural styles of the 18th and 19th centuries. The Marigny, the French Quarter, and Treme are all within walking distance of this road. ◉ *Map K5*

8 Soniat House

A beautifully appointed hotel with the intimate feel of an inn, Soniat House is spread over three historic town houses built in the 19th century. Each room is individually decorated with rare antiques and fine fabrics sourced from all over the world. This gives

Landscaped grounds in Washington Square

the hotel a unique character and elegance. ✪ *1133 Chartres St.* • *Map L5* • *504-522-0570* • *www. soniathouse.com*

9 Lower Decatur Street
One of the liveliest streets in the French Quarter, Lower Decatur Street is lined with eclectic clubs and cafés. These include the laid-back Jimmy Buffett's Margaritaville *(see p44)*, which offers live music and seafood specials, and the upscale fine-dining spot, Palm Court Jazz Café *(see p93)*. Vistors can also grab a good bargain at the French Market or its adjoining flea market. ✪ *Map L5*

Seafood and books on sale, French Market

10 The French Market
Located at the edge of the Mississippi, the French Market has existed at the same site since 1791. Boasting a variety of entertainment, shopping, and food, it is one of the city's most popular shopping areas. Browse through the Flea Market *(see p92)*, which sells everything from clothes to antiques. The Farmer's Market, where local farmers sell fresh produce and seafood, was constructed during the refurbishment of the French Market in 1937–38. Surrounding the main market are smaller stores, restaurants, galleries, and bars. ✪ *1008 North Peters St.* • *Map L6* • *504-522-2621* • *Call for timings* • *www. frenchmarket.org*

A Day in the Lower French Quarter

Morning

🕐 Start your day early at the venerable **Café du Monde** *(see p54)*, where the big attraction is the coffee and *beignets (see p54)*. From there take a walk down **Decatur Street** to the **Farmer's Market**, where you will meet Louisiana farmers who come every morning before sunrise to sell their fresh vegetables, fruit, seafood, and more. Make your way through the market till you reach the community **Flea Market**, which offers some of the greatest shopping in the city. Meander through aisles stocked with original works of art, jewellery, used books, New Orleans souvenirs, and more. Walk over to **Marigny Brasserie** *(see p93)*, where you can enjoy the freshest of ingredients sourced from local farmers and fishermen, and prepared in authentic Creole fashion.

Afternoon

After lunch, make your way back to Barracks Street near the exit to the French Market, where you can see the **Old U.S. Mint** *(see p92)*, built in 1835. This is now part of the **Louisiana State Museum** *(see pp36–7)* where exhibits record Louisiana's past and include the history of jazz, a collection of musical instruments, and an archive of rare documents. After you leave the mint, shop at the boutiques along Decatur Street, but make sure you end the day with some soulful jazz and excellent food at **Palm Court Jazz Café** *(see p93)*.

Left **Cornstalk Hotel** Center **Central Grocery** Right **Gallier House Museum**

🔟 Best of the Rest

1 Cornstalk Hotel
The 19th-century cornstalk fence is the distinguishing feature at this charming, Victorian-style hotel *(see p15)*.

2 Central Grocery
This store has been around since 1906. It is famous for inventing the iconic *muffuletta* *(see p51)*. ⌀ 923 Decatur St. • Map L5 • 504-523-1620 • Closed Sun–Mon

3 Madame John's Legacy
An authentic 18th-century Creole mansion, Madame John's Legacy is one of the buildings that make up the Louisiana State Museum *(see pp36–7)*. ⌀ 632 Dumaine St. • Map L5 • 504-568-6968 • 9am–3:30pm Tue, Wed & Fri; 9am–8pm Thu • http://lsm.crt.state.la.us

4 Joan of Arc Maid of Orleans Statue
This gleaming bronze statue of Joan of Arc Maid of Orleans was a gift from the French. ⌀ St. Philip St. at Decatur St. • Map L5

5 Lafitte's Blacksmith Shop
Originally a late-18th-century tavern, Lafitte's Blacksmith Shop is one of the oldest buildings in New Orleans. Today, it is also one of the hottest bars in the city *(see p28)*.

6 Beauregard-Keyes House and Garden
Built in 1826, this house is named for Confederate general P.G.T. Beauregard and author Frances Parkinson Keyes. It features raised center-hall architecture *(see p68)*. ⌀ 1113 Chartres St. • Map L5 • 504-523-7257 • 10am–3pm Mon–Sat • Adm • www.bkhouse.org

7 Gallier House Museum
James Gallier, Jr. was one of the most prominent 19th-century architects in New Orleans. His elegant Victorian home is now a museum showcasing the architecture of the period *(see p15)*.

8 Old U.S. Mint
A part of the Louisiana State Museum, this mint was used by the Federal government as well as the Confederates. ⌀ 400 Esplanade Ave. • Map L6 • 504-568-6993 • 9:30am–4:30pm Tue–Sat • Adm • http://lsm.crt.state.la.us

9 Frenchmen Street
Located just across from the French Quarter corner of Esplanade and Decatur, this street comes alive after dark with its many fantastic jazz clubs offering a variety of music and late night restaurants. ⌀ Map K6

10 Flea Market
One of the biggest attractions in the French Market, the Flea Market is a delightful place. This sprawling market sells everything from antiques to old records. ⌀ 1008 North Peters St. • Map L6 • 504-522-2621 • 9am–6pm daily • www.frenchmarket.org

Above **A live jazz performance at the Palm Court Jazz Café**

TOP 10 Places to Eat

1 Stella!
Chef Scot Boswell has created a fantastic fine-dining experience, focusing on modern global cuisine. Try the excellent Canadian lobster risotto. 🕲 1032 Chartres St. • Map L5 • 504-587-0091 • $$$$$

2 Muriel's Jackson Square
This opulent restaurant excels in seafood dishes such as wood-grilled Atlantic salmon with bok choy. 🕲 801 Chartres St. • Map L5 • 504-568-1885 • $$$$$

3 Maximo's Italian Grill
A sophisticated Italian eatery with a cozy interior, Maximo's is famous for its divine slow-cooked sauces. 🕲 1117 Decatur St. • Map L5 • 504-586-8883 • $$$$$

4 Mona Lisa
The *Mona Lisa* prints on the wall and the delicious pizza are the chief draws at Mona Lisa. Non-pizza lovers can try the pastas, sandwiches, salads, and delicious desserts. 🕲 1212 Royal St. • Map K5 • 504-522-6746 • $$

5 Angeli
An understated and hip late-night dining spot, Angeli is a favorite among locals and the after-hours bar crowd. The restaurant has an eclectic menu and must-try items include spicy wings, burgers, salads, and specialty pizzas. 🕲 1141 Decatur St. • Map L5 • 504-566-0077 • $$

6 Palm Court Jazz Café
The live jazz music by the legends in the field and Creole themed menu will compel you to return to this place. 🕲 1204 Decatur St. • Map L5 • 504-525-0200 • Closed Mon–Tue • $$$$$

7 Marigny Brasserie
This chic and bright restaurant has a seasonal menu with the freshest ingredients. 🕲 640 Frenchmen St. • Map K6 • 504-945-4472 • $$$$

8 Praline Connection
As well as delicious pralines, this quaint place serves Creole "soul food." Do try their seafood stuffed peppers. 🕲 542 Frenchmen St. • Map K6 • 504-943-3934 • $$

9 Sukho Thai
Authentic Asian fare is Sukho Thai's forte. Choose from their noodle entrées and curry dishes. 🕲 1913 Royal St. • Map K5 • 504-948-9309 • Closed Mon • $$

10 Fiorella's
Local delights, such as seafood gumbo *(see p51)* and fried chicken (which many say is the best in the city), are specialties here. 🕲 1136 Decatur St. • Map L5 • 504-553-2155 • $

Left **Jackson Square** Center **A Bourbon Street Bar** Right **Napoleon House**

Upper French Quarter

THE OLDEST PART OF THE CITY, *this area was built by Jean-Baptiste Le Moyne de Bienville as a French colony in 1721. The architecture is dominated by the combined French and Spanish influences. Although the historic buildings and cultural sights are a big draw, it is the people who command the most attention. The characters on the street are ever-changing and different kinds of performance art can be seen at nearly every corner: silver-painted gymnasts, ballerinas, mime artistes, tap dancing children, and fantastic street musicians are common in this part of the city. Although highly commercial and tourist-centered, the Upper French Quarter is also home to some of the grandest residences, best restaurants, and most vibrant nightclubs and bars in the city.*

Street musicians on Royal Street

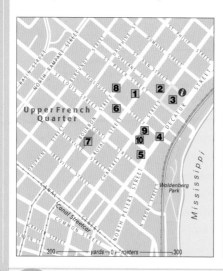

🔟 Sights

1. Royal Street
2. St. Louis Cathedral
3. Jackson Square
4. Jackson Brewery
5. Jean Lafitte National Historical Park Visitor Center
6. Historic New Orleans Collection
7. Royal Sonesta Hotel
8. Bourbon Street
9. Pharmacy Museum
10. Napoleon House

1 Royal Street

One of the most popular streets for shopping in the country, Royal Street offers exquisite antique shops, fine jewelry stores, famous restaurants, and sophisticated cocktail bars. The renowned art galleries on Royal Street attract collectors from all over the world. Some distinctive

Visitors watching entertainers on Royal Street

architecture, including the French Quarter's grandest mansions, can be seen here. Each afternoon, street musicians and performers entertain visitors *(see pp14–17)*.

2 St. Louis Cathedral

Located in Jackson Square, St. Louis is the oldest continuously active Roman Catholic cathedral in the country. Originally constructed in 1727, it was lost to a great fire, but rebuilt in the mid-19th century. The breathtaking interior is well maintained by the Archdiocese of New Orleans. Behind the church is an elegant garden that has an imposing statue of Jesus. After dark, spotlights illuminate the statue, projecting a giant shadow on the back wall of the church, adding to its ambience.

Ⓢ 615 Pere Antoine Alley • Map M4
• 504-525-9585 • Tours: 1–4pm Wed–Sat
• www.stlouiscathedral.org

Imposing spires of St. Louis Cathedral

3 Jackson Square

Originally a central square used for meetings and public executions, Jackson Square has been landscaped and developed into a beautiful garden. It is adjacent to the St. Louis Cathedral and the Pontalba Buildings, which are the oldest apartments in the country. Right in the center of the square is an impressive statue of former U.S. president Andrew Jackson, dedicated to his victory at the Battle of New Orleans in 1815. Along the perimeter are restaurants and novelty shops, all facing out to the artists, fortune tellers, palm readers, and musicians who work in the square *(see pp24–5)*.

4 Jackson Brewery

Also known as The Shops at Jax, Jackson Brewery is a converted brewhouse that is over 110 years old. It is home to four floors of stores, including Big Easy T-Shirt Company and Gumbo Kids. Among the restaurants, bars, and cafés are C's Seafood and Jazz Sushi Bar. The Jax Collection is a small museum-cum-shrine on the second floor, which is dedicated to the history of Jax beer.

Ⓢ 600 Decatur St. • Map M4 • 504-566-7245 • 10am–7pm daily • www. jacksonbrewery.com

Haunted Hotel
Rumors of ghosts float about the Hotel Monteleone <i>(see p14)</i>. Guests and staff have reported doors opening on their own, elevators stopping on the wrong floor, and ghostly images of children. It is on the list of most haunted hotels in the country.

Jean Lafitte National Historical Park Visitor Center

The Visitor Center is a great place for a quick education on the geography, history, and culture of the Mississippi River Delta region. It is also the departure point for daily tours. The Jean Lafitte National Historical Park consists of six sites in Louisiana, all offering guided tours by park rangers. ✪ 419 Decatur St. • Map M4 • 504-589-3882 • 9am–5pm daily

Historic New Orleans Collection

The history of New Orleans goes back about three centuries, and the Historic New Orleans Collection is the pre-eminent collection of archives on the city. It began with the contribution of a personal collection of materials in 1966, but has since expanded into a full-fledged state-of-the-art resource center on Louisiana. Today, it hosts exhibits and serves as a facility for researchers. Tours

Historic New Orleans Collection building

and symposia are part of the agenda. ✪ 533 Royal St. • Map M4 • 504-523-4662 • 9:30am–4:30pm Tue–Sat, 10:30am–4:30pm Sun • www.hnoc.org

Royal Sonesta Hotel

The preferred place to stay during Mardi Gras, the Royal Sonesta is one of those old, luxurious hotels where service is paramount. It is located on bustling Bourbon Street and houses an elegant restaurant, Begue's, as well as an oyster bar and cocktail lounge called Desire. People still dress up to go to the Royal Sonesta, and vie for guest rooms overlooking Bourbon Street <i>(see p29)</i>.

Bourbon Street

A hotbed of shopping, nightlife, restaurants, clubs, and general entertainment, Bourbon Street is one of the liveliest thoroughfares in town. At night it is closed to traffic, so crowds can walk right down the middle of the street. Liquor laws allow drinking on the streets, so all the bars serve drinks to go. A night on Bourbon

Grand central lobby at the Royal Sonesta Hotel

Street can take visitors from club to club, dancing, drinking, and partying *(see pp28–9)*.

9 Pharmacy Museum

The largest museum of pharmaceutical memorabilia in the country, the Pharmacy Museum is located in the building that was home to the first licensed pharmacist in the country. Inside is a collection of artifacts, including medical instruments from the Civil War and a fascinating exhibit about epidemics of the 19th and early 20th centuries. ✆ *514 Chartres St. • Map M4 • 504-565-8027 • 10am–5pm Tue–Sat • Adm • www.pharmacy-museum.org*

10 Napoleon House

Napoleon House was the home of Nicholas Girod, mayor of New Orleans from 1812 to 1815. He planned to free Napoleon from imprisonment at St. Helena Island and bring him here. Although Napoleon died before the mission was completed, the building is still adorned with Napoleonic memorabilia. Today, it houses one of the city's most atmospheric bars, famous for its signature cocktail, the Pimm's Cup. The cupola on the roof is a landmark. ✆ *500 Chartres St. • Map M4 • 504-524-9752 • www.napoleon-house.com*

Napoleon House, with its distinctive roof

A Walk Down Bourbon Street

Early Evening

🕐 The best time to start a walk around Bourbon Street is early in the evening, with a visit to **Bourbon House Restaurant** *(see p29)*, where the oyster bar is among the best in the city. It serves oysters on the half shell from 4 to 6pm daily with specially priced wines by the glass. After happy hour, head down the street for a fantastic dinner at the legendary **Galatoire's Restaurant** *(see p28)*, famous for its soufflé potatoes *béarnaise* and crabmeat specialties.

Nighttime

Dinner is a leisurely affair at Galatoire's, so when you leave it will be way after dark and the perfect time to head to **Chris Owens Club** *(see p28)*, for the most electrifying one-woman show by the owner, Chris Owens. The timings often vary, so call and make reservations for the late show. Thereafter you can stroll further down Bourbon Street, stopping at the various clubs. If you feel adventurous, explore your singing talent at **Cat's Meow Karaoke Club** *(see p28)*. This is a street where the party never stops and there are bars and nightclubs every few yards. However, to make a night of it do stop by the **Famous Door** *(see p28)*, which has an outstanding nightly R&B show band, and the **Old Opera House** *(see p100)*, which does not offer opera, but is a treat for music lovers, offering all-night jazz performances by local acts.

Left **A Gallery of Fine Photography** Center **Martin Lawrence Gallery** Right **Bee Galleries**

🔟 Art Galleries

1 A Gallery of Fine Photography

A collection of photographs by master photographers such as Ansel Adams and Henri Cartier-Bresson fills this distinctive gallery. ☒ *241 Chartres St.* • *Map M4* • *504-568-1313* • *10:30am–5:30pm Thu–Mon* • *www.agallery.com*

2 Michalopoulos

Colorful, contemporary works by celebrated New Orleans artist, James Michalopoulos, are displayed here. ☒ *617 Bienville Ave.* • *Map M4* • *504-558-0505* • *10am–6pm Mon–Sat, 11am–6pm Sun* • *www.michalopoulos.com*

3 Kurt E. Schon, Ltd.

This gallery has been around in the Upper French Quarter for more than 50 years. Spread over five floors, it boasts an impressive collection of 18th- and 19th-century art. ☒ *510 St. Louis St.* • *Map M4* • *504-524-5462* • *10am–5pm Mon–Fri, 10am–3pm Sat* • *www.kurteschonltd.com*

4 Martin Lawrence Gallery

Specializing in sculpture, paintings, and rare graphics, this gallery features work by new and established artists. ☒ *433 Royal St.* • *Map M4* • *504-299-9055* • *Call for timings* • *www.martinlawrence.com*

5 Rodrigue Studio

Famous for his humorous "Blue Dog" series, George Rodrigue's paintings have become serious collector's items today *(see p14)*.

6 Vincent Mann Gallery

A top destination for French art, this gallery showcases the work of Impressionists and post-Impressionists. ☒ *305 Royal St.* • *Map M4* • *504-523-2342* • *Call for timings* • *www.vincentmanngallery.com*

7 Windsor Fine Art

Works of great masters share space with nationally and internationally renowned contemporary artists in this gallery. ☒ *221 Royal St.* • *Map M3* • *504-568-0202* • *10am–5pm Sun–Wed, 9am–9pm Thu–Sat* • *www.windsorfineart.com*

8 Callan Fine Art

Serious collectors rely on Callan Fine Art for European paintings from 1830 to 1950 covering the Academic Art style, the American Barbizon style, and contemporary works. ☒ *240 Chartres St.* • *Map N4* • *504-524-0025* • *Call for timings* • *www.callanfineart.com*

9 Bee Galleries

Bee Galleries claim to have the largest collection of contemporary art in the South. ☒ *319 Chartres St.* • *Map M4* • *504-587-7117* • *10am–6pm Mon–Sat, 11am–5pm Sun* • *www.beegalleries.com*

10 Galerie D'Art Français

An important selection of 20th-century French art is housed in this gallery. The collection is largely made up of Impressionist works. ☒ *541 Royal St.* • *Map M4* • *504-581-6925* • *Call for timings* • *www.neworleansfrenchart.com*

Around Town – Upper French Quarter

Left **Fifi Mahoney's** Center **The Brass Monkey** Right **Faulkner House Books**

🔟 Shopping

1 Fifi-Mahoney's
In a town that loves fancy-dress costumes, Fifi Mahoney's is the perfect store, offering party wigs, cosmetics, and unique accessories. ✎ *934 Royal St. • Map L5 • 504-525-4343*

2 Fleur de Paris
The only serious millinery store in the South, this European-style boutique also offers couture fashion, exquisite jewelry, lingerie, and a collection of beaded handbags *(see p15).*

3 Jack Sutton Fine Jewelry
Sutton's is a premier fine jewelry destination in New Orleans, offering everything from hip-hop jewelry to diamonds and crystals. ✎ *315 Royal St. • Map M4 • 504-522-0555 • www.jacksutton.com*

4 Moss Antiques
A family-owned antique store, Moss Antiques sells art, china, furniture, chandeliers, and a constantly evolving and diverse inventory of new acquisitions. ✎ *411 Royal St. • Map M4 • 504-522-3981 • www. mossantiques.com*

5 Royal Antiques
Royal Antiques is known for its fine art and furnishings. Shop for mirrors, clocks, and lamps here. ✎ *309 Royal St. • Map M4 • 504-524-7033 • www.royalantiques.com*

6 Erzulie's Authentic Voudou
Part retail store and part spiritual and psychic services center, Erzulie's Authentic Voudou is a place with a whole lot of character. ✎ *807 Royal St. • Map L4 • 504-525-2055 • www. erzulies.com*

7 Maskarade Mask Shop
New Orleanians love masks and this shop provides original, artistic masks, and not just during Mardi Gras but through the year. ✎ *630 St. Ann St. • Map L4 • 504-568-1018 • www. frenchquartermaskstore.com*

8 Bourbon French Parfums
For more than 160 years this tiny French Quarter perfumery has been custom blending fragrances. ✎ *805 Royal St. • Map L4 • 504-522-4480 • www. neworleansperfume.com*

9 The Brass Monkey
One of the French Quarter's most eclectic gift shops, the Brass Monkey boasts an extensive collection of Limoges figurines and miniature boxes. ✎ *407 Royal St. • Map M4 • 504-561-0688*

🔟 Faulkner House Books
This small and charming bookstore is a treat for booklovers. It specializes in first editions and books by renowned American authors *(see p25).*

Left **Cat's Meow Karaoke Club** Center **Pat O'Brien's Bar** Right **Old Opera House sign**

🔟 Nightlife

House of Blues
From regional bands and solo acts to internationally acclaimed jazz, rock, and blues performers, the House of Blues is the last word in live music. ◈ *225 Decatur St. • Map N4 • 504-310-4999*

Chris Owens Club
For almost 50 years, singer and dancer Chris Owens has been wowing the crowds with her nightly performances at this club *(see p28)*.

OZ
Located in the gay district on Bourbon Street, OZ is the premier dance club in the area. There are live shows and the music carries on till the wee hours. ◈ *800 Bourbon St. • Map L4 • 504-593-9491*

Cat's Meow Karaoke Club
Located in a 19th-century building, this lively karaoke club is a non-stop party, offering its guests playlists covering hundreds of songs *(see p29)*.

Irvin Mayfield's Jazz Playhouse
Local jazz prodigy Irvin Mayfield runs this upscale jazz club inside the Royal Sonesta Hotel *(see p29)*. He brings in top acts for jam sessions and solo shows, and promotes upcoming talent.

Famous Door
Since the 1930s, this raucous and popular Bourbon Street bar has been providing live entertainment, including show bands and R&B bands, as well as night-long dancing every day of the week *(see p28)*.

Old Opera House
Open all night, every night of the week, this place often sees famous musicians come in and play a set with the house band well after dark. ◈ *601 Bourbon St. • Map M4 • 504-522-3265*

Pat O'Brien's Bar
The signature multi-liquor "Hurricane" cocktail was invented at this iconic bar, which has been going strong for 75 years. Guests can keep the tall Hurricane glass as a souvenir *(see p28)*.

Chateau Moanet Voila
Fridays are the day to go to Voila, when there is a long happy hour. This club, open almost around the clock, even serves breakfast. Try the Cajun omelet. ◈ *300 Decatur St. • Map N4 • 504-581-2534*

Funky Pirate
This pirate-themed bar offers live performances of New Orleans blues music every night. ◈ *727 Bourbon St. • Map L4 • 504-523-1960*

Price Categories

For a three-course meal for one, with half a bottle of wine (or equivalent meal), taxes, and extra charges.

$	under $25
$$	$25–$40
$$$	$40–$55
$$$$	$55–$70
$$$$$	over $70

Above **The bright interior at Ralph Brennan's Redfish Grille**

🔟 Places to Eat

1 Galatoire's Restaurant
The crown jewel of Bourbon Street, Galatoire's is a historic spot dating back to 1905. It has the liveliest Friday lunch in town. This is also one of the few restaurants left that require a jacket for gentlemen *(see p28)*.

2 Brennan's Restaurant
Old-world elegance, great breakfasts, and classic Cajun cuisine served in a beautiful courtyard are the highlights here *(see p14)*.

3 Arnaud's
This upscale place offers Creole cuisine: try the spicy shrimp Arnaud. After dinner, visit the Mardi Gras museum on the second floor. ⊗ *813 Bienville St. • Map M3 • 504-523-5433 • $$$$$*

4 G W Fins
This seafood restaurant stands out for its distinctive dishes, such as blackened swordfish. ⊗ *808 Bienville St. • Map M3 • 504-581-3467 • Closed Sun–Mon • $$$$*

5 Dickie Brennan's Steakhouse
Chic and clubby, this steak house is all about fine cuts of red meat, full-flavored dishes, and perfectly shaken martinis. ⊗ *716 Iberville St. • Map M3 • 504-522-2467 • Closed for L except Fri • $$$$$*

6 Bourbon House Restaurant
This restaurant boasts an outstanding oyster bar and excellent Creole preparations, such as crabmeat-stuffed Gulf fish *(see p29)*.

7 Acme Oyster House
Fresh, hand-shucked Louisiana oysters, cold on the half shell, or char-grilled with sizzling garlic butter, are the house specials. ⊗ *724 Iberville St. • Map M3 • 504-522-5973 • $$*

8 Ralph Brennan's Redfish Grille
The menu at Ralph Brennan's features Gulf of Mexico seafood and spicy Creole specialties. ⊗ *115 Bourbon St. • Map M3 • 504-598-1200 • $$$*

9 Mr. B's Bistro
Casual elegance rules at Mr. B's. Try their wood-grilled fish with mashed potatoes, and a white chocolate brownie with ice cream for a perfect evening meal *(see p15)*.

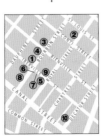

10 Café Giovanni
Authentic Italian cooking and live opera singing three nights a week make this a very romantic spot. The pastas are a must-try. ⊗ *117 Decatur St. • Map N4 • 504-529-2154 • Closed for L • $$$$*

STREETSMART

NEW ORLEANS' TOP 10

Left **A tourist office in New Orleans** Right **Various books on New Orleans**

TOP 10 Planning Your Trip

1 Tourist Offices
The New Orleans Metropolitan Convention & Visitors Bureau can help organize a trip to New Orleans, and the Louisiana State Office of Tourism is a great resource for the rest of the state. The website www.new-orleansonline.com is the official tourism site of New Orleans. ✎ *New Orleans Metropolitan Convention & Visitors Bureau: 2020 St. Charles Ave. • Map J4 • 800-672-6124 • www.nomcvb.com*

2 Internet
There are quite a few websites with a wealth of information about New Orleans. These include www.cityofno.com; www.neworleans.com; bestofneworleans.com; www.nola.com; www.mynewyorleans.com; and www.louisiana.gov.

3 Maps
You can pick up free maps at tourist offices and at major attractions. Each neighborhood has a distinctive layout. The French Quarter, which is essentially a square, is fairly easy to navigate. Other areas, such as Faubourg Marigny or Treme, are a bit more complicated.

4 Passports and Visas
The visa rules for New Orleans are the same as in the rest of the country. Canadian citizens require only proof of residence. Citizens from Visa Waiver Program countries can travel to the U.S. without a visa if they meet certain requirements. However, they must present a passport at the U.S. port of entry.

5 Embassies and Consulates
Contact the U.S. embassy or consulate in your country if you have any queries about visiting New Orleans, or if you need information on current visa requirements.

6 Insurance
It is wise to take out travel insurance before traveling. Policies can cover cancelled flights and lost baggage, in addition to medical expenses. If you have health insurance at home, save receipts from any medical expenses incurred during your trip.

7 When to Go
May through October are the hottest months of the year. October is the busiest convention month, when the city is crowded and hotel rates are highest. November and December have milder weather and great deals on hotels.

8 What to Take
New Orleans is largely casual. There are only a few restaurants that require a jacket. Take light, cotton clothes and comfortable shoes, since you will probably walk about during your trip.

9 How Long to Stay
One week is a good length of time to stay in New Orleans and visit all the major sights in the city. An extended stay might allow for some great excursions.

10 Background Reading
Gumbo Tales: Finding My Place at the New Orleans Table by Sara Roahen gives a glimpse of local culture. John Kennedy Toole's *A Confederacy of Dunces* is a good introduction to the unique neighborhood culture.

Public Holidays
Jan 1
New Year's Day
Jan 19
Birthday of Martin Luther King, Jr.
Third Mon in Feb
Washington's Birthday
Tuesday before Lent
Mardi Gras
Last Mon in May
Memorial Day
Jul 4
Independence Day
Second Mon in Oct
Columbus Day
First Mon in Sep
Labor Day
Nov 11
Veterans Day
Fourth Thu in Nov
Thanksgiving Day
Dec 25
Christmas

Preceding pages **Canal streetcar in front of the World Trade Center**

Left **Airport shuttle** Right **Group director addressing a tour group**

🔟 Getting to New Orleans

1 By Air
All major U.S. airlines offer domestic and international flights to New Orleans. The Louis Armstrong International Airport is modern, efficient, and well-managed. The luggage claim areas are downstairs, as are the exits to all ground transportation facilities and services. The airport is located about 15 miles (24 km) from downtown New Orleans.

2 Amtrak Trains
Three major Amtrak trains serve the city – City of New Orleans, from Chicago; Crescent, from New York's Penn Station; and Sunset Limited, from Orlando or Los Angeles. All make stops at major cities.

3 Greyhound Buses
Greyhound buses serve New Orleans from almost 4,000 locations throughout the U.S. The city's Greyhound bus station is well located on the edge of the Central Business District. It is close to most major Warehouse District and downtown hotels.

4 Car
Driving to the city from any part of the US is a great way to see the countryside as well as move about at your own pace. However, visitors must keep in mind that once in the city, parking can be a challenge.

New Orleans is diligent in its patrols of parking meters and parking tickets are quite common.

5 Customs
Each visitor is allowed to bring in $100 worth of gifts, 0.26 gallons (one liter) of liquor, and 200 cigarettes. Cash or any negotiable funds exceeding $10,000 must be declared. Agricultural items are not allowed through customs and will be confiscated.

6 Shuttles
The most economical way to travel from the airport to New Orleans hotels is via the airport shuttle which can be accessed on the lower level of the airport. Each passenger is allowed up to three bags at no extra charge.

7 Tour Planning
The best way to tour New Orleans is by taking the short area-specific tours. The Garden District offers architectural and historic cemetery tours, while the French Quarter offers ghost tours, architectural tours, and cocktail tours. Research these beforehand and make necessary arrangements upon arrival.

8 Destination Management Companies
These companies arrange trips for groups of visitors. They take care of the

transportation to and within the city, lodging, food, and entertainment. Groups are generally assigned a director who manages the itinerary for the whole trip.

9 Advance Booking and Reservations
During peak convention months (September to November) it may be difficult to get reservations in your preferred hotels, unless you book far in advance. It is easier to get rooms during the summer months, but the weather may not be ideal for traveling.

10 Tour Groups
Joining a group that is traveling to the city can be a fun experience. Do so through travel companies in your originating city. However, you will most likely want to schedule some time independent from the group to explore destinations that hold particular interest for you.

Left **New Orleans cab** Center **The famous New Orleans streetcar** Right **Paddlewheel steamboat**

Getting Around New Orleans

By Car
Getting around New Orleans can be quite challenging, due to heavy traffic and limited parking spaces. Visitors usually find it more convenient to take public transportation, including cabs and the streetcar. Some hotels allow guests to park their cars for a fee that ranges between $20 to $40 per day.

By Bus
Mostly used by locals, the New Orleans bus system, while inexpensive, is often crowded and noisy. Some visitors find buses to be a less than ideal mode of local transportation.

By Cab
Cabs are a good way to get around New Orleans because they are readily available and efficient. You can access cabs in front of your hotel, or flag one down from most downtown streets. If you order a cab by telephone, it will usually show up within a few minutes.

By Streetcar
Streetcars are a great way to get around in New Orleans, and a really nice mode of transportation to truly see the city. Streetcars move at a moderate speed and stop frequently, allowing passengers to see the sites and even take photographs along the way.

By Bicycle
Very few streets in the city have paths reserved for cyclists, which makes safety precautions all the more important. Observe stoplights and stop signs along the way and stay as close to the curb as possible while riding. Riding bicycles at night is not advisable.

By Foot
New Orleans is a great city to see on foot. Walking allows you to stop and study the architectural details of historic buildings, and to shop from the hundreds of small businesses. Walking at night is safe, but stay on the busy streets. Avoid small side streets and poorly lit areas.

By Steamboat
Paddlewheel steamboats still circuit the Mississippi River around New Orleans. A great way to spend an evening is on a dinner cruise up the river. If you are in town for New Year's Eve, seeing the fireworks from the river is an experience not to be missed.

By Limousine
Limousine companies are plentiful in New Orleans, and rates are competitive with most major U.S. cities. You can hire limos for individual trips to one destination, or for an entire day or evening. The business is

popular in the city, so try and book as far in advance as possible.

By Ferry
The ferry that runs from the CBD to the West Bank of New Orleans accommodates pedestrians and cars. It moves very slowly across the river making for a pleasant and relaxing trip. No charge for pedestrians and bicycles.

By Carriage
One of the most enjoyable ways to see the French Quarter is from a horse-drawn carriage. Carriages can be found around Decatur Street, near Jackson Square. The drivers will regale you with historical anecdotes as you travel.

Directory

Buses and Streetcars
• *Regional Transit Authority (RTA):* 504-248-3900; www.norta.com

Cabs
• *United Cab Company:* 504-522-9771; www.unitedcabs.com

Steamboat
• *Steamboat Natchez:* 504-586-8777; www. steamboatnatchez.com

Limousines
• *Nicoll's Transportation:* 504-566-7799; www. neworleanshummer-limousine.com

Left **A busy New Orleans street** Right **Sign for a restricted parking area**

🔟 Things to Avoid

1 Side Streets
New Orleans is generally a very friendly city, but as with any other major urban area, the city has its share of street crime. The best way to stay safe is to travel in reasonably populated areas and busy streets. Avoid poorly lit areas and sparsely inhabited side streets.

2 Driving Frustrations
Traffic moves very slowly in busy parts of the city, especially the CBD and the French Quarter. The best way to get around is on foot, but if the distance is too great, consider a cab. Driving in New Orleans can be frustrating and difficult, and parking spaces are very few.

3 Car Theft
While car theft is not a huge issue in New Orleans, it is always wise to park in brightly lit areas where there are a lot of people. Also, be sure you always close your windows and lock your car when you park. Avoid leaving valuables inside the car.

4 Heat
A trip to New Orleans is far more enjoyable between November and May, simply because of the weather. The average temperature even in October in New Orleans is above 85°F (30°C), and the humidity is quite high. If possible, plan your trip somewhere between Thanksgiving (end of November) and Memorial Day (end of May) when the weather is milder.

5 Water Contamination
Most restaurants in the city offer a choice of bottled water as well as tap water. Some locals drink tap water, but most prefer filtered, cleansed water. In studies done by Tulane University, the local tap water was found safe to drink, but local bottled water companies still do big business.

6 Smoking
Smoking is not legal in restaurants in New Orleans, unless the restaurant is attached to a bar. Most bars ban smoking inside their establishments. Offices and government buildings, schools, and hospitals all ban smoking indoors. It is common to see a lot of people smoking outdoors in the city.

7 Midday Sun
Even in months that offer mild weather, the midday sun in New Orleans can be oppressive. From about 1pm to 3pm, the sun is intense, so do take precautions to avoid prolonged exposure. Dehydration can be a problem, so drink plenty of fluids. Apply sun screen, cover your head, and wear sunglassess.

8 Restricted Parking Areas
The New Orleans Police Department is vigilant in its pursuit of drivers who park in no-parking areas. Parking in a zone reserved for vehicles owned by disabled persons can result in expensive citations. Be careful about keeping parking meters filled with quarters, because ticket writers roam the streets through the day.

9 Panhandlers
Many cities have an abundance of homeless people and New Orleans is no exception. Avoid contact with panhandlers and beggars and those who are obviously intoxicated. They are rarely aggressive but it is still a good idea to avoid confrontation. Always keep your possessions firmly in hand or secure.

10 Walking Late at Night
New Orleans is a late night town, but use good judgment in walking the streets way after dark. If there are still a lot of people on the street where you are walking, go ahead. But if the street is deserted, or sparsely populated, or if you feel insecure for some reason, it is always best to hail a cab.

Left *The Times-Picayune* Center **Newspaper vending machine** Right **Copies of** *Where Y'At*

TOP 10 Sources of Information

1 New Orleans Convention & Visitors Bureau

The NOMCVB is a comprehensive source of information about tourism, general city updates, entertainment, retailers, vendors, and anything that locals or tourists may need to know about the city. It is of great use to people planning travel to New Orleans (see p104).

2 WHERE New Orleans Magazine

WHERE is a monthly periodical especially published for tourists that includes very useful and accurate directories for shopping, dining, lodging, and entertainment. Most hotels in New Orleans offer *WHERE* free of charge in the lobby area. This magazine is essential reading with your guidebooks and other resource materials.

3 New Orleans Magazine

This monthly lifestyle magazine is a part of the New Orleans Magazine group which publishes multiple periodicals, all based on different aspects of life in the city. *New Orleans Magazine* is the flagship publication, while others focus specifically on theater, sports, weddings, and more. The magazine is available in local newsstands and drug stores.

4 The Times-Picayune

The only daily newspaper in New Orleans is *The Times-Picayune*. The paper has been awarded several Pulitzer prizes, and has been publishing in the city for more than a century. *The Times-Picayune* is available at all local newsstands, coffee shops, and with most retailers.

5 NOLA.com

NOLA stands for New Orleans, LA. NOLA. com is the digital component of *The Times-Picayune*, and is updated regularly through the day and night. While the newspaper's content is included on the site, NOLA.com also publishes original content about local, national, and international news events.

6 The Gambit

The Gambit is New Orleans' most prominent alternative newspaper, published weekly in tabloid size. It covers politics, music, entertainment, and theater and also publishes long-form feature stories about topics of interest to local citizens. It is ideal for visitors who want to know what is happening during their visit.

7 NewOrleans online.com

This website is a product of New Orleans Tourism Marketing Corporation, an entity that works to promote the city as a leisure destination. www. neworleansonline.com is one of the most accurate and frequently updated websites about the city, and is also one of the most inclusive providing all kinds of information.

8 Where Y'At

Since the city has such a vibrant and ever-changing music and entertainment scene, this magazine covers, reviews, and offers schedules of all local public events. Music lovers should definitely have a copy of *Where Y'At* during their visit, as it goes into greater detail about scheduled shows than most publications.

9 Louisiana Office of Culture, Recreation, and Tourism

The tourism office of Louisiana maintains a great website, a must for all prospective visitors to the state. ⊛ *www. louisianatravel.com*

10 Regional Transit Authority

Public transportation in New Orleans is the job of the Regional Transit Authority (RTA). The RTA maintains, schedules, and runs all buses and streetcars. Streetcar schedules are available through the RTA. ✆ *504-248-3900* • *www. norta.com*

Left **French Quarter Postal Emporium** Center **U.S. postal service van** Right **One dollar coin**

Streetsmart

🔟 Banking and Communications

1 ATMs
Automatic Teller Machines (ATMs) are located in all parts of the metropolitan area at banks, grocery stores, various retailers, and in many restaurants and bars around town, mainly in the French Quarter. You may incur a fee for completing a transaction at a bank where you do not have an account. Check with your bank for fee schedules.

2 Banking Hours
Most banks in New Orleans have ATMs outside their buildings, which allow 24-hour access. Bank lobby hours in New Orleans run from approximately 9am to 4pm, although some do operate until 5pm. Some banks have drive up windows that operate later than their lobby hours. Call the bank to check exact hours.

3 Traveler's Checks
The use of debit and credit cards has made traveler's checks less popular. Their face value is equal to cash if you buy them in dollars, but you need to present a photo ID, and cashing them in banks or currency exchange offices can be time consuming.

4 Exchange
International visitors should exchange some money before traveling to New Orleans. Look for currency exchange offices in the ticketing lobby of the Louis Armstrong International Airport (see p105). Foreign currency can be exchanged at Mutual of Omaha located in the airport's western lobby. Ⓢ Mutual of Omaha: 900 Airline Drive, Kenner, LA • Map B2 • www. mutualofomaha.com

5 Post Offices
Most U.S. post offices operate from 9am to 5pm on weekdays. Some have secure lobby areas with postal machines that are open till later. Some branches, depending upon their location, stay open on Saturdays for three to four hours in the morning.

6 Internet
There is no shortage of Internet cafés in New Orleans, and most feature wireless connections for laptop users. Ask staff members for information about charges. Some have free service, while others have a minimal charge. Wireless Internet service is available at public libraries. You can also try the French Quarter Postal Emporium or the FedEx Kinko's shops. Ⓢ French Quarter Postal Emporium: 1000 Bourbon St. • Map L4 • 504-525-6651 Ⓢ FedEx Kinko's: 762 and 6823 St. Charles Ave. • Map P3 and Map B5 • 504-581-2541 and 504-525-6651

7 Courier Services
The most popular overnight mailing services are FedEx Express, UPS and DHL. Also consider using the competitively priced U.S. Postal Service for overnight, second, or third day deliveries. In town, there are a number of local courier services that will deliver packages within the city.

8 Phone Cards
If you do not have a long-distance service on your cell phone, you can purchase a phone cards at any of the retailers located all over the city. If you do not have a cell phone, purchasing a phone card may reduce the long-distance charges on your hotel telephone.

9 Hotel Phones and Cell Phones
Generally, using your cell phone will be far less expensive than making calls from your hotel phone. Check with your service provider for details on roaming and long-distance charges. Most big U.S. cell-phone service providers have offices in New Orleans.

10 Postal Services
The U.S. Postal Service provides various services including postage, shipping, change of address, post office boxes, and national and international mail pickup and delivery.

Left **Street musicians on Royal Street** Center **Parking signs with rates** Right **Grocery store**

🔟 Budget Tips

Neighborhood Restaurants

New Orleans is a city full of small, independently owned restaurants. Dining in neighborhood cafés outside of the French Quarter or Central Business District is generally less expensive. Also, there are plenty of delis and fast food stands that provide meals that are quite filling and cheap.

Airline Deals

The airline industry, while highly competitive, is also steadily increasing fares. Flying to New Orleans for a weekend is less expensive if you stay over a Saturday night. Check online travel sites for deals. You might find lower priced tickets if your travel dates are flexible.

Internet Hotel Discounts

Most hotels would prefer you to book online, as it saves them the time and expense of processing the booking. Discounted rates and package deals are often offered on the hotels' websites, that you will not be offered by telephone or in person upon check-in. Study the websites thoroughly for discounted offerings.

Free Museum Days

Free admission to area museums varies from one museum to another. Contact the individual properties or check the websites for admission discounts. Senior citizens and students are sometimes offered certain discounts on admission.

Coupons

Check alternative New Orleans newspapers such as *Where Y'At*, *The Gambit*, and the daily *Times-Picayune* for money-saving coupons. You may find coupons for local entertainment venues, retailers, and restaurants. Many area restaurants feature special discounts during slow travel seasons.

Free Entertainment

New Orleans often has free events and concerts. During certain parts of the year there are afternoon or early evening concerts in public parks, and at other times the city or private organizations sponsor annual festivals. NOLA.com has a full listing of festivals in the website's entertainment section.

Street Performers

New Orleans is a haven for all kinds of artistes including street performers. Musicians, dancers, mimes, jugglers, and magicians can often be found on French Quarter street corners, performing for contributions. Jackson Square is a colorful sight for visitors with Cajun bands, palm readers, tea-leaf readers, and local portrait artists all offering their services for a price.

Parking

Parking is a continual challenge in New Orleans, not only in the busy tourist areas, but even in the residential areas. Watch for signs that specify parking regulations, because they are strictly enforced by the New Orleans Police Department. Public parking lots and garages in heavily-traveled areas can be expensive.

Self-Guided Tours

Area museums often feature self-guided tours of specific exhibits. Some will offer recordings and headsets to guide you. A well-researched trip can yield enough information for you to plan your own self-guided tours of area neighborhoods, historic cemeteries, and architectural attractions.

Grocery Stores

There are surprisingly few large supermarkets in New Orleans. You will, however, find a plethora of corner neighborhood markets. In residential neighborhoods outside of the French Quarter and the Warehouse District, these markets can be an economical way to shop for necessary items. Markets in tourist areas, however, can be expensive.

Left **A thrift shop in the French Quarter** Center **Carnival masks on sale** Right **Antiques on display**

🔟 Shopping Tips

1 Flea Markets
New Orleans flea markets are great places to shop. The French Quarter Flea Market *(see p92)*, located in the lower quarter near the Mississippi River, is open every day, but really comes to life on weekends. Here, you can find just about anything from antiques to vintage clothing and rare books.

2 Antique Shops and Bargaining
Area antique dealers run the gamut from fine, rare inventories to hole-in-the-wall junk shops. Most of the smaller antique dealers will negotiate prices on many, if not most items. This often has much to do with the state of the local economy and the level of tourism at the time you arrive.

3 Thrift Shops and Vintage Stores
Retail stores that feature old or used merchandise that is not necessarily classified as antiques can often be found during a stroll through the French Quarter. Such stores are not often found in other parts of the city, and can be a great place to pick up bargains.

4 Duty Free Shopping
The Louisiana Tax Free Shopping (LTFS) program was the first program of its kind initiated by a U.S. state. The program offers international visitors the opportunity of tax-free shopping while traveling within the state. The program applies to those who can show a foreign passport, an international travel ticket, and who will be in the country for less than 90 days. Designed to promote tourism, the LTFS involves more than 900 participating retailers throughout Louisiana, including all the stores in the airport. Refunds and information can be obtained at the Tax Free Counter, located in the main lobby of the main terminal of the international airport *(see p105)*.

5 Store Hours
There is no local standard for retail store operating hours. The hours in local stores vary as widely as the types of merchandise they carry. Generally, most stores open between 9am and 10pm, but some independently owned stores do not always honor their posted hours.

6 Department Stores
New Orleans has very few large department stores. Small businesses are the rule in here, as the economy is driven more by independently-owned businesses. In large shopping malls there are a few department stores, mostly of national chain retailers.

7 Souvenir Stores
The French Quarter is awash with souvenir and t-shirt stores and local packaged food stores with items indigenous to the area. Prices are generally a bit high for these items, based on what the tourist market will bear.

8 Shipping
Many retailers in the city offer shipping assistance with the merchandise you purchase in their stores. If you are purchasing items that you clearly cannot carry with you, such as furniture or art objects, inquire first about shipping services and rates, before you make the purchase.

9 Refunds
Each seller has its own refund and exchange policy. Usually these policies are stated in writing somewhere in the store. If not, find out about the store's policy from the salesperson or manager. If the store is part of a national chain, you may be able to return merchandise in other cities as well.

10 Sales Tax
Retail purchases made in the city of New Orleans are subject to a combined sales tax of 9 percent, which includes 4 percent state sales tax and 5 percent city sales tax.

Left **Visitors on Segways** Right **Streetcar with wheelchair access**

TOP 10 Special Needs Tips

1 Wheelchair-Accessible Streets

Most streets in downtown New Orleans and the French Quarter are wheelchair accessible. However, other parts of the city are inconsistent in their accessibility. Many streets have never been fully repaired after the 2005 hurricanes, and may be difficult to negotiate. Check with your hotel concierge for more information.

2 Wheelchair-Accessible Buses

Extensive features, such as kneeling capability, lifts, wheelchair-securement areas, and priority seating, ensure equal access on the fixed-route buses of New Orleans. These buses under the Mobility Impaired Transit System (MITS) provide curb-to-curb service and access for ambulatory riders with disabilities, or those using assisting devices, such as walkers, canes, or crutches.

3 Wheelchair Accessible Streetcars

The fixed-route streetcars may be difficult to negotiate for people with disabilities. The red Canal streetcar is wheelchair accessible while the green St Charles streetcar is not. Consult the New Orleans Regional Transit Authority (see p108) website for detailed information on

"Para-Transit" eligibility. This is a special program for those unable to use the RTA fixed-route system independently.

4 American Disability Act

Consult the Americans with Disabilities Act (ADA) website for information on laws pertaining to people with physical limitations. 🔊 www.ada.gov

5 Disabled Parking

New Orleans has fixed parking spaces for the disabled. Almost every public parking lot has an allotted space for those with physical disabilities. Individuals without certification will be fined for parking in these spaces. 🔊 To obtain relevant documents call: 504-483-4610

6 Wheelchair-Accessible Hotels

Most hotels in New Orleans comply with the ADA requirements and have rooms with wider doorways, floor-level accessible showers, and other features that make life easier for those with disabilities. Contact the hotel in advance for more details about the property.

7 Airport Facilities

The Louis Armstrong International Airport is free of architectural barriers, making it accessible to wheelchair-users. For the hearing

impaired, there are Telephone Display Devices (TDD) located throughout the airport. Visual Paging and Flight Information Display monitors are also available all over the airport premises. 🔊 Main TDD no: 504-463-1057

8 Scooter Tours

Mobility scooters, powerchairs, Segways, and wheelchairs are available on rent for disabled visitors as well as senior citizens who would like to take a relaxed self-guided tour of New Orleans. A typical tour route takes a minimum of 3 hours and can include highlights of the French Quarter and the riverfront. 🔊 www.cityscootertours.com; www.scootaround.com

9 Wheelchair Rental

There are many medical supply companies that rent out wheelchairs and other equipment for the disabled. Consult your hotel concierge for information on the medical-equipment vendors they work with. 🔊 www.mrwheelchair.com

10 Services for the Blind

The Lighthouse for the Blind is a non-profit organization offering a variety of programs to help blind and visually impaired individuals of all age groups. 🔊 504-899-4501 • www.lhb.org

Left **Royal Pharmacy, Royal Street** Center **Police officer** Right **Pedestrian crossing**

🔟 Security and Health

1 Hospitals and Urgent Care Centers

New Orleans is a health care hub. It has a number of highly rated hospitals, including Tulane University Medical Center, Ochsner Medical Center, and East Jefferson General Hospital. 🟢 *Ochsner Medical Center: 1514 Jefferson Hwy. • 504-842-3210* 🟢 *Tulane University Medical Center: 1415 Tulane Ave. • Map B5 • 504-988-5800* 🟢 *East Jefferson General Hospital: 4200 Houma Boulevard Metairie • 504-454-4000*

2 Pharmacies

Pharmacies are located in most hospitals and drug stores across the city. The popular pharmacies include Walgreens stores, CVS drugstores, and Walmart stores. All the pharmacies are staffed with licensed pharmacists. Travelers from another state or abroad must bring their insurance documents if buying medicines.

3 Natural Hazards

Hurricanes in the city are infrequent but devastating. In case of such an emergency, follow the announcements on local television and radio. Also check the National Hurricane Center's forecasts online at www.nhc.noaa.gov. Visitors should also protect themselves against the sun by wearing a hat, using sunscreen and drinking plenty of fluids.

4 Emergency Services

The 911 emergency line is strictly for situations requiring immediate attention. For police, fire, or ambulance, dial 911. Stay on the line even if you are unable to speak so that the emergency operator system can track you. Emergency calls are free.

5 Police

The New Orleans Police Department has three divisions: one on foot, a second on motorcycles, and a third in patrol cars. All three patrol the city streets, especially in busy tourist areas, and there is a strong police presence 24 hours a day. 🟢 *Police Department 504-821-2222.*

6 Pedestrian Crossings

Pedestrian crossings are clearly marked in most parts of New Orleans. Some crossings have lights that say "walk" or "don't walk," but others do not. Pedestrians should be careful while crossing major thoroughfares and exercise caution during rush hour.

7 Seat Belt Law

Drivers of cars, vans, and trucks, as well as all passengers in the front and back seats of the vehicles, must wear a seat belt at all times while the vehicle is moving. State and local law-enforcement officers are aggressive in implementing this law and issue citations for those who do not comply.

8 Driver Safety

In New Orleans, city officials have gone to great lengths to ensure traffic safety. As a driver, be aware that many intersections have traffic cameras that will automatically video tape and photograph your car and send traffic tickets in the mail for speeding.

9 Embassies and Consulates

As a major urban center, New Orleans has a number of consulates from countries across the world. Non-U.S. citizens should contact their embassy or consulate for any kind of legal assistance.

10 Security and Safety in Hotels

In the major hotels, security is an absolute priority and there are very few incidents of crime or other antisocial behaviour. In smaller, boutique hotels visitors should keep their valuables safe and exercise caution, especially while coming in and going out late at night. The same is true of bed and breakfast inns.

Left **A Lucky Dog hot dog cart** Center **Dress code sign** Right **A bar on Bourbon Street**

Accommodation and Dining Tips

1 Restaurants
There are many high-end restaurants run by celebrity chefs in New Orleans, which offer traditional Cajun and Creole delicacies, as well as innovative cuisine. There are also theme cafés and bistros serving Italian, Mediterranean, and other specialties. For cheaper options such as the famous po'boys or muffulettas (see p51), walk into a deli or a grocery store.

2 Early Bird Dinners
Some restaurants in New Orleans offer discounted menus or "early bird dinners," which take place prior to the usual meal time and consist of three-course dinners at a reduced price. Look for these cheaper, fixed-price specials during slow tourist months.

3 Vegetarian Food
There is no dearth of variety in this city that loves its food. Vegetarian travelers can eat at any of the Thai, Vietnamese, or exclusive vegetarian restaurants. Although Creole and Cajun food is primarily meat based, most chefs can whip up a delicious meat-free meal on request.

4 Proper Restaurant Attire
Although casual attire is acceptable in most restaurants in the city, there are still a few places that require a jacket and tie. Smart-casual clothing is advised for upscale restaurants, while more informal attire, such as shorts, are acceptable in others.

5 Fast Food
American fast food outlets are located at nearly every street corner. Major franchise-based restaurants such as Wendy's, McDonald's, and Burger King have multiple outlets. There are also local restaurants offering Cajun-Creole and Italian fast food, as well as numerous corner stores offering a variety of sandwiches. Visitors should also look out for the famous Lucky Dog hot dog carts in the French Quarter.

6 Tipping
Tipping in New Orleans follows the standards of most major cities in the country. It is courteous to tip between 15 and 20 percent in restaurants. Tips for drivers are generally at the discretion of the passenger, but rarely go below 10 percent.

7 Alcohol
The legal drinking age in New Orleans is 21. Alcohol can be purchased 7 days a week and there are no laws dictating how late a bar should be open. It is also legal to drink in plastic cups while walking on the streets, however, glass bottles are prohibited. Most bars in New Orleans have takeaway options for all drinks on the menu.

8 Online Bookings
A large number of hotels, car services, tour operators, and destination-management companies (see p105) offer discounted rates on the Internet. On hotel websites, look for the "Internet Only" section.

9 Motel Chains
There are quite a few motel chains in New Orleans, but they are usually located in the suburbs, rather than in the city proper. Because of their remote locations, the rates may be lower, but transportation to and from these motels may be problematic for some travelers.

10 Extended-Stay Facilities
Some major hotel chains have extended-stay properties in and around New Orleans. These offer weekly and monthly rates. Rooms include full kitchen and laundry facilities. There are also some all-suite hotels, which offer apartments with fully equipped kitchens and independent sitting rooms. These also offer Internet and Wi-Fi facilities and are perfect for business as well as leisure travelers.

Price Categories

For a standard double room per night during tourist season, including taxes and service charges.

$	$50–$100
$$	$100–$150
$$$	$150–$200
$$$$	$200–$250
$$$$$	over $250

Left **Degas House** Center **Dauphine House**

⑩ Bed and Breakfast

1 House on Bayou Road

A National Register plantation house dating back to 1798, this building has been restored as a quiet bed and breakfast. Cooking classes by top chefs from New Orleans restaurants are also on offer here. ✆ 2275 Bayou Rd • Map E2 • 504-945-0992 • www.houseon-bayouroad.com • $$$$

2 Degas House

French Impressionist Edgar Degas actually stayed and painted in this building. Today, it is a meticulously maintained bed and breakfast on one of the most picturesque streets in the city. ✆ 2306 Esplanade Ave. • Map E2 • 504-821-5009 • www.degashouse.com • $$$$

3 Melrose Mansion

This huge Victorian Gothic-style mansion was built in 1884, to house a single family. Luxurious, private, and imbued with an old world charm, Melrose Mansion features one of the most romantic suites in the city. ✆ 937 Esplanade Ave. • Map K5 • 504-944-2255 • www.melrosemansion.com • $$$

4 Dauphine House

Built in 1860, Dauphine House has hardwood floors, high ceilings, and is just around the corner from the French Quarter. This well-kept property has rooms available for less than $100 for most months of the year. ✆ 1830 Dauphine St. • Map K5 • 504-940-0943 • www.dauphinehouse.com • $$

5 Claiborne Mansion

The Claiborne Mansion, located in the Faubourg Marigny, is one of the most elegantly restored mansions in the area. The property is designed to make guests feel like they are staying in a private home. ✆ 2111 Dauphine St. • Map K6 • 504-949-7327 • www.clairbornemansion.com • $$$$$

6 Ashton's Bed & Breakfast

This 10,000-sq-ft (930-sq-m) Greek Revival mansion has been lovingly transformed into a bed and breakfast. The main house features high ceilings, spacious rooms, and fine period furnishings. ✆ 2023 Esplanade Ave. • Map E2 • 504-942-7048 • www.ashtonsbb.com • $$$

7 Chimes Bed & Breakfast

An uptown inn that has been around since 1986, Chimes Bed & Breakfast oozes historic charm. The inn has all the modern conveniences, such as Wi-Fi. Each of the five rooms have French doors opening on to a common courtyard. The rooms also have their own private entrance. ✆ 1146 Constantinople St. • Map C6 • 504-899-2621 • www.chimesneworleans.com • $$$

8 Avenue Inn

This beautiful house is located among ancient oak trees on the street-car line and dates back to 1891. Guests can choose from a wide variety of rooms. ✆ 4125 St. Charles Ave. • Map C6 • 504-269-2640 • www.avenueinnbb.com • $$$$

9 Sully Mansion

This Garden District mansion, designed by famous New Orleans architect Thomas Sully in 1890, has just eight guest rooms and is in close proximity to the St. Charles streetcar line. High ceilings and a wrap-around porch give this place the feel of old New Orleans. ✆ 2631 Prytania St. • Map H5 • 504-891-0457 • www.sullymansion.com • $$$

10 Lafitte Guest House

Located in the heart of the French Quarter, this restored property has richly-decorated rooms that are filled with antiques from around the world. The building dates back to the mid-19th century. ✆ 1003 Bourbon St. • Map L4 • 504-581-2678 • www.lafitteguesthouse.com • $$$

Left **Ambassador Hotel** Center **Bienville House** Right **Parc St. Charles**

Mid-Range Hotels

1 O'Keefe Plaza Hotel

A basic, clean, and centrally located hotel offering astoundingly low prices, the O'Keefe Plaza has 129 rooms with modern facilities. Some also have kitchenettes. ⊛ *334 O'Keefe Ave. • Map N2 • 888-524-8586 • www. okeefeplazahotel.com • $*

2 Ambassador Hotel

Originally a warehouse, this hotel has a modern and minimalist look. The Ambassador is located within walking distance of Harrah's New Orleans Casino *(see p30)*, Riverwalk Marketplace, and the Ernest N. Morial Convention Center *(see p21)*. It retains the exposed brick walls and high ceilings from the old building. The wrought-iron furniture completes the look. Some of the rooms have Jacuzzis. ⊛ *535 Tchoupitoulas St. • Map P4 • 800-455-3417 • www.ambassadorhotel neworleans.com • $$$*

3 Bon Maison Guest House

This 19th-century town house has been refashioned into a guest house built around a beautiful courtyard. Located just walking distance from the French Quarter, this hotel has simple rooms with all modern conveniences. ⊛ *835 Bourbon St. • Map L4 • 504-561-8498 • www. bonmaison.com • $$*

4 Le Richelieu

This hotel is popular with travelers who regularly visit the city. The well-kept property is also centrally located. ⊛ *1234 Chartres St. • Map L5 • 504-529-2492 • www. lerichelieuhotel.com • $$$*

5 Parc St. Charles

Situated on one of the busiest downtown corners, Parc St. Charles is a clean and utilitarian hotel. It is within walking distance of the riverfront and the St. Charles streetcar. ⊛ *500 St. Charles Ave. • Map P3 • 504-522-9000 • www. parcstcharles.com • $$*

6 St. Charles Inn

A well-maintained hotel, the St. Charles Inn is located in a busy part of town. The St. Charles streetcar stops outside the front entrance, providing easy access to most city attractions. Good restaurants dot the surrounding area. ⊛ *3636 St. Charles Ave. • Map C6 • 504-899-8888 • www.bestwestern louisiana.com • $$*

7 Avenue Plaza Resort

This all-suite hotel bills itself as a resort with a swimming pool and fitness facilities. All the rooms reflect an old-world charm and have their own kitchenettes. ⊛ *2111 St. Charles Ave. • Map J4 • 504-566-1212 • www. avenueplazaresort.com • $$*

8 Bienville House

The lobby of this charming hotel has marble floors and sparkling chandeliers. The rooms are large and luxurious. Try to reserve a balcony room overlooking the elegantly landscaped pool area and courtyard. ⊛ *320 Decatur St. • Map N4 • 504-529-2345 • www.bienvillehouse. com • $$$*

9 Columns Hotel

The grand front porch of the Columns Hotel is an ideal place to enjoy cocktails while watching the streetcar rumble by. Listed in the National Register of Historic Places, this Italianate building was designed by famous New Orleans architect, Thomas Sully. Although the rooms are a little old fashioned, the moderate pricing makes it worth your while. The main advantage is the hotel's scenic location. ⊛ *3811 St. Charles Ave. • Map C6 • 504-899-9308 • www. thecolumns.com • $$$*

10 Comfort Inn & Suites Downtown

This hotel is located in the center of the CBD and within walking distance of the French Quarter. It needs some sprucing up but still offers good accessibility and a great bargain. ⊛ *346 Baronne St. • Map N2 • 504-524-1140 • www. comfortinn.com • $$*

Streetsmart

Price Categories

For a standard double room per night during tourist season, including taxes and service charges.

$	$50–$100
$$	$100–$150
$$$	$150–$200
$$$$	$200–$250
$$$$$	over $250

Hilton Riverside Hotel

🔟 Business Hotels

1 Hotel Inter-Continental
This is the preferred hotel for business travelers who visit the city regularly. The rooms are large, and well-equipped with modern workspace accessories. Restaurants and lounges are elegant and comfortable. ✪ 444 St. Charles Ave. • 504-525-5566 • Map N3 • www.ichotelsgroup.com • $$$

2 Sheraton New Orleans Hotel
Its bright, spacious, and well-equipped rooms, modern amenities, good restaurants and bars, and central location ensures a loyal clientele. The hotel has five majestic ballrooms and 54 individual meeting rooms. ✪ 500 Canal St. • Map N4 • 504-525-2500 • www.sheratonneworleans.com • $$

3 Hilton Riverside Hotel
This is the largest hotel in New Orleans and is designed for business travelers and holiday-makers alike. Located on the banks of the Mississippi, it is especially convenient for business travelers heading to the Ernest N. Morial Convention Center; it is just down the block. The rooms are spacious and very well-appointed. ✪ 2 Poydras St. • Map P4 • 504-561-0500 • www1.hilton.com • $$$

4 Loews Hotel
This hotel features some of the largest rooms in the city. No expense has been spared on the furnishings, lighting, and art adorning the walls. There is a modern business center and teleconferencing facility. ✪ 300 Poydras St. • Map P4 • 504-595-3300 • www.loewshotels.com • $$$$

5 Doubletree Hotel
The Doubletree is walking distance from the downtown area, the French Quarter, and the Warehouse District. Rooms are spacious with modern conveniences. The hotel's restaurant is mediocre, but there are several good eateries nearby. ✪ 300 Canal St. • Map N4 • 504-581-1300 • www.neworleans.doubletree.com • $$$

6 Renaissance Pere Marquette
Built in 1925, this historic downtown hotel has been beautifully renovated and is now a luxurious property with stylish decor. ✪ 817 Common St. • Map N3 • 504-525-1111 • www.marriott.com • $$$$

7 Hampton Inn & Suites
Located within a five-minute walk of the Ernest N. Morial Convention Center, this hotel offers a fully equipped business center and free Wi-Fi service. The decor is in the French-Colonial style and the complimentary breakfast buffet is an added plus. ✪ 1201 Convention Center Blvd. • Map R4 • 504-566-9990 • www.neworleans hamptoninns.com • $$$$$

8 Hilton Garden Inn – New Orleans Convention Center
Located just across from the Morial Convention Center, this modern property has a relaxed ambience and restaurant serving American classics. ✪ 1001 S. Peters St. • Map R4 • 504-525-0044 • http://hiltongarden-inn1.hilton.com • $$$$

9 Hyatt Regency New Orleans
This property overlooks the Mercedes-Benz Superdome (see p74) and has around 2,000 guest rooms. The hotel includes an extensive meeting and exhibit space. ✪ 601 Loyola Ave. • Map P2 • 504-561-1234 • www.neworleans.hyatt.com • $$$$

10 Harrah's New Orleans Hotel
Harrah's is one of the newest hotels in the city. It features state-of-the-art business equipment and is located on a busy inter-section in the downtown area. ✪ 228 Poydras St. • Map P4 • 504-523-6000 • www.harrahsneworleans.com • $$$$$

Left **Royal Sonesta Hotel** Center **St. James Hotel** Right **Omni Royal Orleans**

🔟 Vintage Hotels

1 Lamothe House Hotel

This hotel provides a truly vintage New Orleans experience. Lamothe House Hotel is an artfully refurbished 19th-century mansion located within walking distance of the major attractions in the French Quarter. ✆ *621 Esplanade Ave. • Map K5 • www.lamothehouse.com • 800-367-5858 • $$$*

2 Royal Sonesta Hotel

The large 500-room Royal Sonesta combines a rich heritage along with completely modern amenities. Located on a busy Bourbon Street corner, the hotel is home to Begue's, one of New Orleans' most highly regarded restaurants. ✆ *300 Bourbon St. • Map M4 • 504-586-0300 • www.royalsonesta.com • $$$$$*

3 Omni Royal Orleans

This hotel, located in the center of the French Quarter, is an elegant and beautifully maintained property. It houses the gourmet restaurant, Rib Room, which is a carnivore's delight. ✆ *621 St. Louis St. • Map M4 • 504-529-5333 • www.omnihotels.com • $$$*

4 Le Richelieu

A favorite with regular visitors to the city, Le Richelieu is surprisingly quiet despite its bustling French Quarter location. Rates are moderate, compared to similar properties in the area. ✆ *1234 Chartres St. • Map L5 • 504-529-2492 • www.lerichelieuhotel.com • $$$*

5 Cornstalk Hotel

Famous for its charming cornstalk-shaped cast-iron fence, this hotel is a converted 19th-century home. With only twelve beautifully furnished rooms, the hotel is both charming and intimate. ✆ *915 Royal St. • Map L5 • 504-523-1515 • www.cornstalkhotel.com • $$$*

6 Frenchmen Hotel

An early-19th-century town house, which has been authentically restored to its original splendor, Frenchmen Hotel is located in the French Quarter. Rooms are decorated with period furniture and equipped with all modern amenities. ✆ *417 Frenchmen St. • Map K6 • 800-831-1781 • www.frenchmenhotel.com • $$$$*

7 St. James Hotel

Housed in the 19th-century trading center, Banks Arcade, St. James Hotel has a charming West Indian decor throughout its 86 guest rooms. It is home to the famous Cuvee restaurant. ✆ *330 Magazine St. • Map P4 • 504-304-4000 • www.saintjameshotel.com • $$$*

8 Le Pavillon Hotel

Le Pavillon is one of the few remaining hotels boasting a majestic lobby with 40-ft (12-m) ceilings, chandeliers, and a grand dining room. The whole place has a distinct old-world charm. Rooms are well-appointed, and the service is exceptional. ✆ *833 Poydras St. • Map P2 • 504-581-3111 • www.lepavillon.com • $$$$$*

9 St. Peter's House

Situated right in the heart of the French Quarter, this building dates back over a century and has served as a hotel for many years. St. Peter's House has central courtyards and broad iron-lace balconies lending the hotel a flavor of the old South. Each of the 29 rooms are individually decorated with carefully selected antique furniture. ✆ *1005 St. Peter St. • Map L4 • 800-535-7815 • www.stpeterhouse.com • $$$$*

10 Prince Conti Hotel

Although the Prince Conti has all the modern conveniences you would expect, the ambience is that of a stylish 19th-century French chateau. Rooms are elegant and the service is great. It is also home to the stylish Bombay Club, which serves fine Creole food. ✆ *830 Conti St. • Map M3 • 800-366-2743 • www.princecontihotel.com • $$$*

Left **Ritz-Carlton Hotel** Right **Soniat House**

TOP 10 Luxury Hotels

1 Windsor Court Hotel

Some consider this the city's finest contemporary hotel. It boasts an excellent art collection, plush rooms, as well as one of New Orleans' finest dining spots, The Grill Room *(see p52)*. ⊗ *300 Gravier St. • Map N4 • 504-523-6000 • www. windsorcourthotel.com • $$$$$*

2 W New Orleans – French Quarter

The smaller, boutique-style sister of the W Hotel New Orleans has a charming courtyard and tastefully decorated rooms. The outdoor pool is heated and surrounded by trees. ⊗ *316 Chartres St. • Map M4 • 504-581-1200 • www.wfrench quarter.com • $$$$$*

3 Ritz-Carlton Hotel

The Ritz-Carlton name generally signifies excellence. This particular hotel is located in an artfully renovated historic building, which was once a department store. The rooms are among the finest in the city and the service is impeccable. ⊗ *921 Canal St. • Map M3 504-561-0500 • www. ritzcarlton.com • $$$$$*

4 W Hotel New Orleans

The W offers modern elegance with a hip vibe. The hotel decor is minimalist, the amenities upscale and luxurious.

The W is known for its absolute privacy. ⊗ *333 Poydras St. • Map P2 • 504-525-9444 • www. whotels.com • $$$$$*

5 Westin Canal Place

This hotel, overlooking the Mississippi, spells sheer grandeur with an elegant dining room, a beautiful lobby with large French windows, and spacious and well-appointed guest rooms. ⊗ *100 Iberville St. • Map N4 • 504-566-7006 • www. westin.com • $$$$$*

6 International House Hotel

The rooms at this hotel are comparatively small, but beautifully appointed. The lobby is redecorated four times in a year, with the changing of the seasons. Loa, the hotel lounge, is one of the hippest bars in town. ⊗ *221 Camp St. • Map N3 • 504-553-9550 • www. ihhotel.com • $$$*

7 Soniat House

Built in 1829, Soniat House has the intimacy of a private home. The staff pay attention to details and each room is individually decorated with fine furnishings. Many travelers consider this among the best hotels in New Orleans and it is a favorite with visiting celebrities. ⊗ *1133 Chartres St. • Map L5 • 504-522-0570 • www. soniathouse.com • $$$$$*

8 Roosevelt Hotel New Orleans

This historic hotel originally opened as the Grunewald in 1893. It was given a new life after renovations by the Waldorf Astoria Collection. The lobby has marble floors and elegant gold-leaf columns. The hotel's legendary Blue Room, where jazz greats like Louis Armstrong and Ray Charles used to perform, hosts jazz brunches every Sunday. ⊗ *123 Baronne St. • Map N3 • 504-648-1200 • www.therooseveltnew orleans.com • $$$$$*

9 Hotel Monteleone

The *grande dame* of the traditional New Orleans luxury hotels, the Monteleone boasts sublime guest rooms and suites, restaurants, and a spa. The hotel is rumored to be haunted, but that does not seem to have affected its popularity. ⊗ *214 Royal St. • Map M3 • 504-523-3341 • www.hotelmonteleone. com • $$$$*

10 Lafayette Hotel

A historic landmark dating back to 1916, this hotel has been restored to its original splendor. Its period decor is complemented by the French doors and wrought-iron balconies. The St. Charles streetcar stops just outside. ⊗ *600 St. Charles Ave. • Map P3 • 800-366-2743 • www. thelafayettehotel.com • $$*

General Index

Acknowledgments

The Author
Paul A. Greenberg is a journalist and professor who has lived in New Orleans for the past 25 years. He decided to make the city his permanent home because of its rich culture, history, and outstanding food. He has written for regional and local publications and authored several travel guides.

Photographer Helena Smith
Additional Photography Peter Anderson; Dave King; Rough Guides: Greg Ward.
Fact Checker Christopher Thacker

At DK INDIA
Managing Editor Aruna Ghose
Editorial Manager Sheeba Bhatnagar
Design Manager Kavita Saha
Project Editors Diya Kohli and Souvik Mukherjee
Project Designer Namrata Adhwaryu
Assistant Cartographic Manager Suresh Kumar
Cartographer Zafar-ul-Islam Khan
Senior Picture Research Coordinator Taiyaba Khatoon
Picture Researcher Shweta Andrews
DTP Coordinator Azeem Siddiqui
DTP Designer Rakesh Pal
Indexer Amit Kapil
Proofreader George Theimi

At DK LONDON
Publisher Douglas Amrine
List Manager Julie Oughton
Design Manager Mabel Chan
Senior Editor Sadie Smith
Project Editors Alexandra Whittleton, Dora Whitaker
Senior Cartographic Editor Casper Morris
DTP Operator Jason Little
Production Controller Mandy Inness

Design and Editorial Assistance
Louise Cleghorn, Karen D'Souza, Lydia Halliday, Kaberi Hazarika, Shikha Kulkarni, Paul Oswell

Picture Credits
Key:
a-above; b-below/bottom; c-centre; f-far; l-left; r-right; t-top.

Photography Permissions
Dorling Kindersley would like to thank the following for their assistance and kind permission to photograph at their establishments:

African American Museum, Audubon Aquarium of the Americas, Audubon Zoo, Authur Roger Gallery, Bee Galleries, Bourbon House Restaurant, The Brass Monkey, Bryant Galleries, Café Degas, Café Lafitte in Exile, Café Rani, Casell Gallery, Contemporary Arts Center, Coquette, Dauphine House, Degas House, Faulkner House Books, Fifi Mahoney's, French Antique Shop, Galatorie's Restaurant, Gallier House, Good Friends Bar, Le Petit Théâtre du Vieux Carré, Louisiana Children's Museum, Maple Leaf Bar, New Orleans Museum of Art, Ogden Museum of Southern Art, Palace Café, Palm Court Jazz Café, Preservation Hall, Ralph Brennan's Redfish Grille, Rodrigue Studio, Royal Sonesta Hotel, Tipitina's.

Works of art have been reproduced with the kind permission of the following copyright holders:

Monument to the Immigrants © Franco Alessandrini 20cb.

Spanish Main 1963 Acrylic on Poplar Wood 60 x 60 x 11 © annetruitt.org / Bridgeman Art Library 9 tl.

The publisher would like to thank the following individuals, companies, and picture libraries for their kind permission to reproduce their photographs:

ALAMY: David Davis Photoproductions 24-25c; Nick Higham 20cb, 102-103; Peter Horree 28-29c; Andre Jenny 72c; Andy Levin 22cla, 60tr; Nadia Mackenzie 22bc; Ninette Maumus 23tr; Simon Reddy 89bl; Peter Titmuss 30-31c; Travel Division Images 57cla; Vespasian 23clb; Wallace Weeks 26br; Paul Wood 22-23c.

AUDUBON AQUARIUM OF THE AMERICAS: 6bl, 19cr, 72tc.

CORBIS: Brad Edelman 60tl; Hemis/ Patrick Frilet 48-49; Ron Kuntz 34tc; U.S. Coast Guard - - digital ve/ Science Faction 35bl.

GETTY IMAGES: Afp/ Staff/ Robyn Beck 23cr; National Geographic/ Tyrone Turner 23cb; Staff/ Mario Tama 22crb; Stringer/ Chris Graythen 32-33.

THE GRANGER COLLECTION, NEW YORK: 34tl.

HOUMAS HOUSE PLANTATION: 62bl.

LAFAYETTETRAVEL.COM: Eric Lindberg 63tr; Lucid images/ Mark Downey 62t.

LOUISIANA SUPERDOME: 74bl.

MARTIN LAWRENCE GALLERY: 98tc.

MASTERFILE: ClassicStock 64-65. MR. B's BISTRO: 52tr.

THE NATIONAL WWII MUSEUM: 42br.

NEW ORLEANS CITY PARK: 27tl.

NEW ORLEANS MUSEUM OF ART: 11cra, 36tl, *Waves* by Lin Emery photo John D'Addario 8br.

NEWORLEANSONLINE.COM: 7tr, 60cl.

PHOTOLIBRARY: Age Fotostock / Terrance Klassen 4-5; Jon Arnold Travel /John Coletti 14-15; James May 61bl; Photodisc/ White 86-87; Superstock/ Richard Cummins 1c.

PRIVATE COLLECTION: 34cra, 35tr.

ST. LOUIS CATHEDRAL: 34tr.

All other images © Dorling Kindersley
For further information see: www.dkimages.com

Special Editions of DK Travel Guides

DK Travel Guides can be purchased in bulk quantities at discounted prices for use in promotions or as premiums. We are also able to offer special editions and personalized jackets, corporate imprints, and excerpts from all of our books, tailored specifically to meet your own needs.

To find out more, please contact:
(in the United States) **SpecialSales@dk.com**
(in the UK) **travelspecialsales@uk.dk.com**
(in Canada) DK Special Sales at **general@tourmaline.ca**
(in Australia) **business.development@pearson.com.au**

Street Index